JUN 1 7 2015

D1230877

MORTGAGES MADE EASY

8 Steps to Smart Borrowing
for Homes and
Investment Properties

BRUCE BRAMMALL

Wrightbooks
A Wiley Brand

INDIAN PRAIRIE PUBLIC LIBRARY
401 Plainfield Rd.
Darien, IL 60561

First published in 2015 by Wrightbooks

An imprint of John Wiley & Sons Australia, Ltd
42 McDougall St, Milton Qld 4064

Office also in Melbourne

Typeset in 11.3/14 pt ITC Berkeley Oldstyle Std

© Bruce Brammall 2015

The moral rights of the author have been asserted

National Library of Australia Cataloguing-in-Publication data:

Creator:	Brammall, Bruce, 1970– author.
Title:	Mortgages Made Easy: 8 steps to smart borrowing for homes and investment properties / Bruce Brammall.
ISBN:	9780730316565 (pbk.)
	9780730316572 (ebook)
	9780730321569 (custom edition)
Subjects:	Mortgage loans — Australia
	Housing — Australia — Finance.
	House buying — Australia — Costs.
Dewey Number:	332.720994

All rights reserved. Except as permitted under the *Australian Copyright Act 1968* (for example, a fair dealing for the purposes of study, research, criticism or review), no part of this book may be reproduced, stored in a retrieval system, communicated or transmitted in any form or by any means without prior written permission. All inquiries should be made to the publisher at the address above.

Cover design by Wiley

Front cover image (trade edition) by © iStockphoto.com/Alexsl

Front cover author photo (custom edition) and back cover author photo (trade edition) by Andrew Tauber

Printed in Singapore by C.O.S. Printers Pte Ltd

10 9 8 7 6 5 4 3 2 1

Disclaimer
The material in this publication is of the nature of general comment only, and does not represent professional advice. It is not intended to provide specific guidance for particular circumstances and it should not be relied on as the basis for any decision to take action or not take action on any matter which it covers. Readers should obtain professional advice where appropriate, before making any such decision. To the maximum extent permitted by law, the author and publisher disclaim all responsibility and liability to any person, arising directly or indirectly from any person taking or not taking action based on the information in this publication.

Genevieve, Edward and Amelia (aka Mrs DebtMan,
DebtBoy and DebtGirl) — with you in my life, even the scariest
deadlines are of little consequence.

Contents

Assumptions and disclaimers

This book has not relied upon any individual's circumstances.

Bruce Brammall is a licensed financial adviser and mortgage broker with Bruce Brammall Financial and Bruce Brammall Lending respectively. However nothing in this book should be taken as individual financial advice and readers should always seek specific financial advice relevant to their own situation before making any decisions or entering into any transactions.

Tax and accounting

The author does not represent himself to be a tax accountant and information in this book should not be relied upon for taxation advice for your individual circumstances.

Information in this book, including tax rates, tax law and stamp duty, are subject to change by governments without notice. You should consult with your accountant to understand how individual strategies would impact on your personal taxation circumstances.

Assumptions

For the most part in this book, where examples have been used, we have used property price growth (or appreciation) of 5 per cent and rental yields of 4 per cent. This gives a total return from property of 9 per cent. In its paper titled 'Is Housing Overvalued?' in July 2014, the Reserve Bank found that rents had maintained a relatively constant rate of 4.2 per cent over the last 60 years. While yields are usually fairly stable, property prices can fluctuate considerably.

We have generally used interest rates that are higher than at the time of writing, when the Reserve Bank of Australia had an official interest rate of 2.5 per cent and the standard variable rates of the major banks were about 5.9 per cent.

The marginal tax rates used in this book are generally going to be those for the 2014–15 financial year. Those marginal tax rates will generally include 2 per cent for the Medicare levy (including the 0.5 per cent for the National Disability Insurance Scheme) and the 2 per cent deficit levy for those earning more than $180 000.

In regards to superannuation, the assumptions used relate to the 2014–15 financial year, including for tax and conditions of release. Governments have speculated that the age at which Australians might be able to access their superannuation could rise in future years.

Regarding chapter 6, on self-managed super funds and gearing property investing: The information on SMSFs and gearing was current at the time of writing. Governments have a habit of fiddling with superannuation rules and it's recommended that readers check current laws before taking action to invest in this space.

About the author

But for a *Sliding Doors* moment—a beach, a bonfire and a passionate moment that I was surprised *not* to be a participant in—me and a mortgage might have become acquainted much earlier in life.

I was to remain a debt virgin for a few years yet. I just know that first near-debt experience would have been very clumsy and awkward. I'm pretty sure I'd have gone against, without knowing, most of the advice contained in this book.

They say maturity makes for a better lover. (Get your minds out of the gutter. I'm still referring to debt.) In 1999, when I was about 28, I quite literally had a book thrown at me. 'Here, want to read this?' It was a book about property investment. A book about property investment is, by default, a book about mortgages. I fell in love instantly. Then I became besotted. That turned into obsession. And I bought my first investment property. It was followed by many more properties, some of which were homes. Hey, turns out obsession isn't always a bad thing.

At the time, I was a journalist at Melbourne's *Herald Sun*. Journalists have free rein to ask whatever questions they've got the gumption to pose of whomever they can get their mugs in front of. (As a bonus, they get to muck around a lot and get invited to places where the beers are normally free.) And if you've got a keen interest in all things financial, the business section of a major metro is the place to be. So I accepted an invitation. When I wasn't writing about Australia's banks, fund managers and insurance companies, I'd be challenging people to extend my knowledge on mortgages and property.

In 2003, I became the deputy business editor of the paper. A few years later, there was another sliding door—witnessing events occurring to colleagues, rather than being a participant—and I chose to walk through it. I started studying to become a financial adviser. As soon as that study project finished, I co-wrote my first property investment book, *The Power of Property* (Wrightbooks, 2006). I left the *Herald Sun* at the end of 2006, after 15 years, for the world of financial advice.

In my first year as an adviser, I authored *Investing in Real Estate For Dummies* (John Wiley & Sons, 2008). The second edition of this book, *Property Investing For Dummies* (2013) also had the spin-off *Getting Started in Property Investing For Dummies* (2013).

The first *For Dummies* title was immediately followed by the book that had been banging around in my head for a few years, *Debt Man Walking: A 10-Step Investment and Gearing Guide for Generation X* (Wrightbooks, 2008) (www.debtman.com.au).

The reaction to *Debt Man Walking* was overwhelming. It forced, in February 2009, the launch of what has since become Bruce Brammall Financial (originally Castellan Financial Consulting). In mid 2012, to assist clients with their property mortgage needs, I launched Bruce Brammall Lending (which was Castellan Lending until September 2014).

The writing bug is a pretty persistent and hungry critter. Actually, it's more like a tapeworm. Thankfully, News Limited (where I'm the Generation X columnist in *Your Money*), *Eureka Report* (where I'm superannuation editor) and *The West Australian* (where I have possibly too much freedom as the *Debt Man* columnist) allow me to feed that voracious beast.

In between the career change, writing columns and books, and launching a few businesses, comes the fun part. Sometimes, not often enough, I get to play husband to Genevieve (the irrepressible Mrs DebtMan) and dad to Edward and Amelia (the gorgeous little DebtKids).

In essence, I get my buzz from educating and informing and, for those who like my writing style, entertaining. I'm a teacher. My classroom is a newspaper, a website, a boardroom or a hall full of people. What I'm hoping is that this book is your *Sliding Doors* moment. That it changes your life, even just a little bit. If the mortgage (and property) advice in *Mortgages Made Easy* helps you into your first home, or your first investment property, then pass it on.

Bruce Brammall

Bruce Brammall Financial Pty Ltd
Debt Man™
BA (Communications), Adv. Dip. (Financial Planning), Cert. IV (Mortgage Broking)
Email: bruce@brucebrammallfinancial.com.au
Twitter: @brucebrammall

Acknowledgements

There is a price to be paid for a book. And hopefully with it comes a reward.

For you, the reader, it's about 30 bucks (depending on whether it's a physical book or e-book) and about 10 to 20 hours of your time. With most books, I think you get your money's worth in enjoyment from the words on the page. But there's an added bonus with finance titles — you can often literally make thousands of dollars out of the ideas in them! Awesome! Many books have done that for me, and I hope *Mortgages Made Easy* does the same for you.

Authors pay a price: blood, sweat and tears. More accurately, writer's angst (blood), deadline panic (sweat) and estrangement from family (tears). All of which happened in the writing of this book. The upside for me? Well, you reading this bit. And moving on to enjoy the rest of this book. Ultimately, I hope that you profit from reading this book. To complete the karmic cycle, contact me to let me know if something from this book made a difference to your life. Authors love it. Hit me with an email: bruce@brucebrammallfinancial.com.au. Or visit the website (www.brucebrammallfinancial.com.au) to sign up for our newsletters or find out some more about the process.

While one person bashes out the words, that's only a part of the story of a book. This book, for instance, wouldn't have happened without the following people's involvement.

My wife, Genevieve. Mrs DebtMan has said 'no' to every book I've ever considered after the first one. But she comes around. Because she's tops. (And because a husband barricaded in his office writing a book is a husband who's not fighting for control of the remote.)

In order of appearance, Edward (DebtBoy) and Amelia (DebtGirl). You might think you love me more than I love you, but that's simply not possible. This fact won't become obvious to either of you for a while. But one day, in about 25 to 30 years, you'll understand.

This book is, in essence, a follow up to *Debt Man Walking*, published in 2008. A lot of unexpected stuff followed *DMW*'s publication. There was the unexpected reaction to the book, which unexpectedly launched a few businesses (Castellan Financial Consulting and Castellan Lending, which morphed into Bruce Brammall Financial in September 2014), which meant that I have met a whole bunch of wonderful people, both clients and friends of the businesses, that I would not have otherwise met.

So, to the fantastic clients of Bruce Brammall Financial, many sincere thank-yous. This book wouldn't have occurred without your incredible support. It's the clients who are attracted to our business' core values—education, protection, simplicity, independence, fairness, leadership and wisdom—who spread the word via referrals, who humble me and my staff every day with their support for our business.

Thanks to Helen Savage, my office manager and first employee, the other woman in charge of managing my time. My life would be an even more hectic and disorganised mess without your continued professional assistance.

Over shorter periods, but for similar reasons, go thanks to Bruce Brammall Financial's other staff, including Gautam 'Gordon' Seth and Ian Wood, without whom the business simply wouldn't be what it is.

I'm only allowed to continue writing books because people were kind enough to pay for and read the previous ones. Thank you to all those who have, as well as those who read my weekly columns in some of Australia's great media publications, including *The West Australian*, *Eureka Report* and News Limited's *Your Money* personal finance section.

With those publications, I've worked with some great editors. Not only have they given me latitude to write with a bit of flair and occasionally let me have a rant, but they are extra special because they approve invoice payments. Honourable mentions there go to James Kirby (*Eureka Report*), Sean Smith and Neale Prior (*The West Australian*) and Anthony Keane (News Limited's *Your Money*).

There was a point in time when I needed a retreat, a writer's log cabin, or else this book wouldn't have happened. The SOS flare went out and to the rescue came Maurn and Anne and way more than a log cabin. Eternal gratitude.

There are places in life that you avoid. They're uncomfortable and irksome. They make you feel jittery and nauseous. For reasons I still can't always fathom, every week I allow my business coach Geoff McDonnell to lead me to these haunted houses. But with a 'creepy places tour guide' like Geoff, they all turn out to be manageable.

And to marketing guru Toby Ralph, for quickly and succinctly ending five years of branding confusion.

Speaking of great mentors, special thanks to two truly fine mortgage brokers, John Frame and Tanya du Preez of Loan Clinic, who are brilliantly knowledgeable and generous with their time.

Kristen Hammond, executive commissioning editor at publisher Wiley, hopefully knows that I think she's awesome for her help with this book and previously with *Debt Man Walking*. Just in case she doesn't, here I go: 'Kristen, you're awesome'.

And for *Mortgages Made Easy*'s editor, Allison Hiew, who literally added wisdom from half a world away, a final special thanks for the many improvements you made to this book.

Introduction

Debt is a four-letter word. And it's going to get a fair run in this book, so if the word offends you, you should gently put this book down now and calmly back away. No one needs to get hurt here.

As a word or concept, debt has got a reputation that rivals some of the other four-letter words that get bleeped on radio and television and that I try really, really hard not to use in front of my children. Honestly.

Most financial commentators and the media seem to have a near pathological fear of debt, without ever actually explaining why it's evil. 'It's bad because, you know, it's, um, not good.' It just seems to be a universally accepted truth that it's evil, like the devil, spam email, mosquitos and Justin Bieber. In post–Global Financial Crisis years, even politicians have been sticking the boot in, demonising government debt and trying to unceremoniously kick it to death.

Debt doesn't deserve its reputation. It's just a tool whose intentions are good. Oh lord, why does it seem so misunderstood? (With apologies to the song made a classic by The Animals in 1965.)

And, no, it's not even fair to think of debt as a 'necessary evil'.

If you want to buy property, debt is simply a necessity. You can't buy real estate without it. Well, most of us can't. And the 1 per cent who can do it without borrowing know how financially smart debt can be, so they usually buy with debt anyway.

Hating it or fearing it won't change the fact that you *need* it to buy property. Given that, if you and debt are going to be hanging together for a while, you might as well learn to get along.

Let's take that one step further. If you take the time to start getting along as buddies ... hey, you might just find out that there's a whole other likeable side to debt. And that side is the role it can play in wealth creation.

Debt makes the word go around. Sure, I know The Beatles reckon it was love. So did KISS, Madonna and, as I've seen more recently, the *Powerpuff Girls*. But they're wrong.

If debt really was evil—like alcohol, cigarettes and petrol—wouldn't it be taxed? Debt actually gets the opposite of that. It's not only not taxed, it will often get you a *tax deduction*. Not all debt, but great debt gets a tax break (and there will be plenty of information on that kind of debt in this book).

Debt is not thine enemy. Debt be thy friend. Or at least a largely obedient pet.

If you want to buy property, you really have to get that. You may be inexperienced with debt, but know that you need to get chummy with it. Or you may already be familiar, but want to get more intimate.

Mortgages Made Easy will teach you what you need to know about debt as it relates to property mortgages, both to own a home and purchase investment property, and even to build a property portfolio.

Regarding mortgages, we'll start off with an education on the role of debt in property, how debt helps you to create wealth with property, and then I'll show you how to get financially fit for your first mortgage.

Then we'll go through the key decision-making process that can lead you to getting a mortgage that will best suit your property purchasing ambitions and, more importantly, probably allow you to get rid of that mortgage sooner. There are plenty of banking products that you can harness for good to do exactly that.

Most importantly, we'll disassemble debt for purchasing property. Too many people think a mortgage is about getting the lowest interest rate you can. A low interest rate is fine, but there are a number of far more important boxes that need to be ticked before worrying about interest rates (which largely gets sorted out by competition).

You also need to know *how to structure your mortgage*. It's critical. And while there are tips throughout the book, there's a whole chapter on making sure you get the structures of both the ownership and your mortgage right.

Just because I'm that sort of guy—and because I've written five books on property investment—I'll also give you dozens of tips on buying property as well.

All property knowledge starts with the understanding that there are only two reasons to buy property. You're either buying a home, or you're buying an investment. The former is about creating financial security for your family. The latter is about making money, pure and simple. How you achieve either of those goals depends on a series of choices about what you're trying to achieve and what route you're going to take to get there.

And I'll even take you through buying property in a self-managed superannuation fund (SMSF), which has only become possible in recent years. It's an exciting (relatively) new development for property investors and, while not suitable for everyone, presents a significant opportunity to improve your retirement savings, for those who understand property already (if the government doesn't change the rules).

While this book is designed to be a guide to allow you to do it yourself, understand that the knowledge that you will gain from this book will only kick-start your process of specific research for getting the right loan for your circumstances.

You might find that you don't have the time to do enough research. If that's the case, give Bruce Brammall Financial a call and we'll save you plenty of time and hassle.

Try www.brucebrammallfinancial.com.au, or call 03 9020 2905.

So, let's get started.

1

Debt—the grease that oils the property wheel

Okay Mouseketeers, this book is talking about money and property, so I want you to start by having a quick look in that place where you stash your cash. So take a second to grab your wallet or purse.

How much is in there? Probably somewhere between $0 and $300. A quick survey of some Facebook friends suggests the average is probably $50. (But a startling number of my mates had less than ten bucks!)

What will chump change of $50 get you? It will fill roughly half of your car's petrol tank, which might get you 300 kilometres out of Dodge. It might get you a new tie, if it's on sale. It might also get you drunk (once). But it won't do much more than that. And it definitely won't do all three. Unless you drive a Vespa, buy your ties at an op shop and are a really cheap drunk.

Clearly, it won't buy you a house.

If you bought this book because you intend to buy property, and you are staring down $50 in your wallet, then your best bet might be to play Monopoly—and fantasise about global domination and making millions.

Or you could track down 13 000 of your closest mates, con them into giving you the $50 in their wallets, and then you could purchase the average Australian house. Got that many mates? You'd have to hold a house-warming with more beer than the fraternity in *National Lampoon's Animal House* to pay them all back.

True, our wallets aren't where we keep most of our cash these days. We're not yet the cashless society predicted a few decades ago, but most of our money sits in bank accounts, where it enters and departs largely electronically. Depressingly, many people have more money in their wallets than they do in their bank accounts.

Since you're reading this book, one thing is certain: you don't intend to let a little problem like a current lack of savings stop you from achieving the 'Great Australian Dream'. No chance.

So you want to buy a property. Is it a home or an investment property you've got your eye on?

Well, I hope this news isn't going to be too disappointing for you, but you can't buy property with cash. Not with your cash, anyway. Not what's in your wallet. Not what's in your bank account. Not even if you were to max out a cash withdrawal from your credit card.

Short of winning the lotto, or having a childless aunty die and leave you her millions, you will never have enough cash in your wallet, or the bank, to be able to buy a home or an investment property.

You can't save your way to a home

I've seen friends try to save their way to buying a home. Well, that's what they seemed to be doing. They saved and saved, for year after year. The more money they saved, the higher house prices went and the bigger the place they wanted as their first home.

They ended up with the biggest deposit I've ever personally known — about a quarter of a million dollars — which had taken them about ten years to save. But over that decade, what they wanted as a home had grown from around $300 000 to about a million bucks.

Yep, had they bought the same home when they had a deposit of $50 000 or $100 000, they probably would have had a mortgage of $270 000 (with a $50 000 deposit), instead of about $800 000 (with a $250 000 deposit).

Simply, you can't save yourself all the way to owning a home. You want to buy property? You are going to need help. You're going to need other people's money. That, dear readers, is going to involve borrowing money.

And assistance on that front would be the point of this book.

Property and borrowing go hand in hand, even more so than love and marriage in Frank Sinatra's classic song of the same name (synonymous for a certain generation with Al and Peg Bundy in *Married… With Children*).

Property comes with debt. Lots of it. It's generally going to be multiples of the combined annual income of you and your partner. For property virgins, it's a total freak-out mountain of debt. Signing up for your first home loan is usually more gut-churning than walking down the aisle, anticipating your HSC results and watching an all-night marathon of Freddy Krueger movies.

Well, it tends to be that scary and come with that level of debt in the beginning at least.

Not helping those fears is the bad-arse reputation that debt comes with, at least part of which is not deserved. (A bit like Ozzy Osbourne. Yes, he bit the head off a bat at a concert in 1982. But no, he didn't realise it was a *real* bat—he thought it was made from rubber.)

If you think debt is a dirty four-letter word, then you need to stop, take a minute and make a decision. Debt is a tool. And unless you're going to save here in Australia and then go and buy in a third-world country, you and debt are going to have to get acquainted.

So, you either need to (a) get over it and accept that property and debt go together like Vegemite and toast, or (b) put down this book and continue renting forever.

The point of *Mortgages Made Easy* is not to try to convince you to take on debt—the reality is you have no choice if you want to own property. The point of this book is to show you how to best make mortgages work for you in your goal of wealth creation via property.

There is no such thing as 'the perfect mortgage'. Some mortgages will suit you. Others won't. The point about mortgage debt is to find a package or solution that works well for you. To do that, you need to understand what mortgages are and how they can and can't be used to make your dream of property ownership and wealth creation a reality.

But before we go on, there is something critical that I need you to understand, which is so often misunderstood by people looking at property for the first time.

Homes versus investment properties

At its most basic, property ownership has two forms. There's owning a property for you to live in (a home). And then there's owning a property for someone else to live in (an investment property). They are both real estate. They can look exactly the same — even be next door to each other.

But they are very, very different. And never the twain *should* meet.

I go into more detail about this in chapter 2. But for now, understand that they are worlds apart. One you will live in; the other you won't. The base reason for buying them should be very different. They are total opposites when it comes to tax. The way you should view them as purchases is different. The way you should spend money on them is different.

We will make the distinction between *home* and *investment property* throughout *Mortgages Made Easy*, while *property* and *real estate* could mean either homes or investment properties.

So why did you pick up this book?

I'm assuming you want one of the two — either a home or an investment property. You might even be thinking ahead and wanting to buy both! Fantastic! I'm a card-carrying nut for property both as homes and investments — this is my sixth book that covers property in one dimension or another — so there will also be plenty of tips on purchasing property in this book.

But the main aim of this book is to explain how to make mortgages and banks work best for you in improving your future wealth through property.

I want you, through reading this book, to gain the confidence to take on debt on your terms and in a way that will help you own your home sooner, or build your wealth via your property portfolio faster. (Or, if you still need help, I will show you how professional mortgage brokers could assist.)

It is crucial to get the debt part of property right. If you do get it right, you can potentially own your home *years* sooner, or make your investment property work thousands of dollars a year better for you.

If you came looking to buy a home, great. Buying your own home is the cornerstone of wealth creation (and we go into more detail on this in chapter 5). People who buy their own home generally end up wealthier than those who rent their whole lives. Getting started might seem hard and the mortgage mountain might seem like a painful hill to climb. I get that. But, like everything in life, including your finances, it's a case of 'no pain, no gain'. There has to be some sacrifice.

If it's investment property you're after, then avoiding the mortgage pitfalls is critical to maximising your investment returns. Getting an investment property wrong can be financially disastrous. And with 15 years of being involved in, and writing about, the property market, I can help save you from some of the property disasters awaiting the unsuspecting.

What's your goal?

As a financial adviser, I see a lot of people who want to improve their finances, but don't necessarily know how to do it. As an author, I know that anyone who buys finance books wants to educate themselves to do the right thing for their finances.

But just thinking and reading won't get you anywhere. Nothing happens without action. If you're reading this book, you're 'in the market'. You just want to make sure you do it right.

You've got two choices. You either arm yourself with enough information to do it yourself. Or you hire good help.

But prior to any of that, you need a purpose. You need to set some goals.

Fear + greed = powerful motivators

The two best motivators in life are fear and greed.

Fear is the emotion that says: 'I don't want to live out my old and cranky years eating baked beans on the age pension.' Anything that drives you to strive for more is a healthy fear, isn't it?

But greed has a reputational issue. The Catholics insist it's one of the seven deadly sins; but Michael Douglas (playing Gordon Gekko in *Wall Street*) told us 'Greed…is good'. When it comes to my own finances, I'm on the side of making sure I can look after myself (and my clients should too). If you want something more out of life, then you'll need at least a hint of greed. Is greed really evil if you're simply trying to create a better life for your family?

Part of that 'better life' can come with property ownership—either via homes or investment properties. And if that's why you picked up this book, then you need to make yourself some promises.

Setting your targets

So, let's cut through the crud. I want you to be certain about why you're doing this.

Plans are worth nothing unless they're written down. So take a minute or two to put them down on paper, then pin them up somewhere you will regularly see them (such as above or beside your computer). Seeing them regularly makes for a powerful reminder every time you sit down to work.

Here are some suggestions:

- getting out of the rental rat race and into home ownership
- paying off my home in 15 years
- buying an investment property
- building a property portfolio that will allow me to retire sooner
- creating a rental income stream to eventually replace my own income

- buying a holiday home for my family

- planning for a wealthier retirement.

Only you can decide what goes on your list. It could be one of these goals, or a number of the ones on that list. Or a whole bunch that you've come up with yourself.

Then be more specific. By what date is your home going to be paid off? How many properties are going to be in your portfolio? At what age do you want to retire? How much passive income do you want from property?

Property has been a great wealth creator over hundreds of years, for millions of people. Those who make property fortunes have inevitably done so by getting the important things right, and avoiding the easy-to-make errors that stand in your way.

What does *getting it right* mean?

Some people will claim that *getting it right* when it comes to property and debt is simply about making sure you get the lowest interest rate.

Nope. Wrong. On so many levels.

Interest rates are one part of the equation. And overpaying a bank anything is wasteful. But to a degree, interest rates are negotiable. And, often, many lenders will match a rate for you.

Just as important is making sure that you have the right 'optional extras' on your property loan to suit your lifestyle and what you're trying to do. These are often the tools that may help you pay down your mortgage faster. Your choice of tools depends on you making some important decisions, such as whether you need offset or redraw accounts, whether interest-only is best for you, and whether you'd benefit from taking on professional packages, free credit cards and fixed versus variable loans. This is covered in great detail in chapters 4 and 8.

Just as importantly, you need to get the ownership structure right at the start. Getting this wrong could be devastatingly expensive. At its worst, poor ownership structure could lead to you losing not just your investment property, but also your family home. (Come home and explain that one to your partner!) We cover this in chapter 8.

Debt is a tool…use it properly

Anyone who is about to pile into debt for property also needs to understand that debt has a dark side. It can be very Jekyll and Hyde.

Borrowing is also known as leverage. And financial 'leverage', as with machines, means that a small effort can have a much larger impact. A bicycle is a machine. It's a lot faster to get around on a bike than it is to walk, for about the same effort.

Leverage is great when markets are going up; not so much when they are going down. And debt can quickly get very dangerous when things get downright ugly in the economy.

Property is a long-term investment. You need to be able to ride out the bumps. You can't control the economy, which moves in cycles, but you need to be able to go the distance with a property investment.

And the biggest tools of all…

Debt can be used in really stupid ways. And so many people get stuck in a rut with debt. Getting out of a bad-debt rut can be difficult, but until people learn to overcome the behaviours that are keeping them in their financial situation, getting ahead will be even harder.

An understanding of the different types of debt is critical to using debt correctly to build wealth. There are three types of debt—*dumb*, *okay* and *great*. And I go into detail on the types of debt in chapter 3.

But we do need to get one thing crystal clear. Right now.

If you have multiple credit cards that are never (or rarely) paid down to $0, if you often buy furniture or electricals using interest-free periods (and don't pay them off in time), if you paid half a year or more in salary for your current car, or avoid family and friends because of how much money you owe them, then you're not using debt the right way. And wealth through property is going to be difficult until you can change those behaviours.

These are all examples of *dumb debt*, and they are consumer traps. The interest rates with these types of debt can be stratospheric. They indicate that you don't understand the difference between *need* and *want*. They suggest that you're living a lifestyle beyond your current income. You're not used to having to deny yourself anything.

If I've just described your current finances, then you might have some work to do on your budget and understanding of savings. (You will find some budgeting tools at www.brucebrammallfinancial.com.au.)

Delayed gratification—money's golden rule

Money has rules. And the truly wealthy understand those rules intimately. The most important money rule of all to understand is the concept of *delayed gratification*.

Delayed gratification is a concept that was tested by American scientist Walter Mischel in the 1960s and 1970s. The professor ran a test on a bunch of four-year-olds. He put them in a room with a marshmallow on the table. These kids were told that if, when an adult came back into the room, the marshmallow was still there, they could have two marshmallows. However, if they ate the one on the table, they wouldn't get a second.

Oh, the humanity! The cruelty to children! What an evil professor! They were just ... Generation X ... babies!

But it showed something really important. Most kids succumbed within minutes. Some just wolfed it down the second the door was closed. Others tried hard to stop themselves—they tried to fall asleep or turned their back on it. Others picked it up, licked it, then put it down again. But 90 per cent ate it.

About 10 per cent of the kids were able to delay their gratification and got two marshmallows. Smart kids. What's a five-minute wait to double the pleasure? Later, the researchers followed up with them. They found that those same kids were more financially successful. They were more likely to have completed university degrees, be wealthier and have more friends, and less likely to have tried drugs.

Delaying gratification is tremendously powerful. Those who can will achieve far greater financial success. It is, in fact, the key to success. If you don't spend that $1 now, you can invest it for your financial future.

Why's that important here? Buying property—whether for a home or for investment—represents delayed gratification, financial strain now in the hope of greater financial rewards later. It is almost certainly cheaper, up to the medium term, to rent a house rather than to have a mortgage on the same house. And much investment property is negatively geared for the first seven to ten or so years of ownership; that is, the owner has to subsidise the person renting the house.

You could spend that money instead. But by understanding the importance of delayed gratification, you can make real, positive changes to your financial future.

But let's move on to chapter 2 and look at why property can be a great asset for your financial future.

Property purchasing principles

All the people I have helped to buy homes or investment properties have either already had some clarity as to what they were looking to achieve, or they were very close. Some people just need to sit down with a financial professional to make sure their property goals are realistic and achievable in the medium to long term.

Property purchases are inevitably big financial decisions that require the right starting mindset. That mindset requires you to have a degree of hunger to improve your financial situation.

And just to ram it home ... here are the key points to take away from this chapter.

- Debt is necessary to buy or invest in property.

- Homes and investment properties are completely different beasts.

- You need to understand your goals before purchasing property.

- Fear and greed are essential factors in gaining a better life.

- The lowest interest rate is not the only factor in deciding which mortgage works for you.

- Dumb debt is disastrous for your future and needs to be addressed before investing in property.

- Delayed gratification is key to financial success.

2

Why property is so popular

Hey, homies! Where are you right now?

If you're reading this book, there's a reasonable chance you're at home. Your home. You might own it. You might not. Either way, it's your home. And home feels kinda good, doesn't it?

Why does home feel so good? Why do we spend so much time there? Why is it that we feel this sense of 'Aaaah ...' when we walk in the front door?

Like they say in *The Castle*, it's about 'the serenity'.

Home is a place where you can chillax and feel safe and just be yourself. It's a place where you set the rules, where you get peace and quiet from the hustle and bustle that happens *out there*. Hopefully it's roughly where you want to live, be that near friends or family, close to work or a great coffee shop, or in the delivery zone for the best pizza in the solar system. It's got a great backyard or courtyard. You love the park across the road, or the fact that your kids' school is a few hundred metres down the road.

Home is not always serene and peaceful. If you've got children (like my DebtKiddies), then it can resemble a zoo, with the various animals screaming at each other. Sometimes it feels like I might have been less stressed if I'd stayed at work. But I wouldn't rather be at work, would I? I'd rather be home.

Home is our safety zone. A place where we love to spend downtime. Where we make home-cooked meals and where our partner or family is waiting for us.

Why invest in property?

Importantly, home is also a place to stash your stuff, and everyone needs a place for that.

That's why property can be such a great investment—demand. There will always be a demand for places to stash one's stuff. Some people want to own their home, while others are happy to pay rent to someone else for that place.

Australians are besotted with property ownership. It's a good thing, too, because we've got plenty of it. We're the sixth-largest country on earth, but there's only 20-something million of us here. We haven't really spread out and we're unlikely to. About two-thirds of us live in just the five mainland capitals of Sydney, Melbourne, Brisbane, Perth and Adelaide. Demand for real estate in those cities is high. And, roughly, it works in ripples from the centre of those cities outwards to regional areas and rural areas and then to the bush, where you can buy land in lots of dozens of hectares at a time.

The power of property

The real power of property comes from the strong underlying demand for what is a limited resource—the land that properties sit on.

The scarcer a resource, the more some will be prepared to pay for it. Do you know how much land there is within a 5 km radius of a capital city post office? Remember your high school maths? The equation is πr^2, with r equalling 5 on this occasion. The answer is 78.54 square kilometres.

That's not really a lot of land. Only so many can live in that area—though high-rise buildings can increase the density. If you're prepared to pay more to live there than someone else, then you can live there, either by buying a property, or paying rent (to an investor).

Obviously, as you go further out, there's more land. When supply is greater, price will generally be lower also.

Two types of property ... don't mistake them

We touch on this in chapter 1, but now we're going to explore in detail why homes and investment properties are actually so different that they're almost opposites.

Too many people buy a home thinking that they are buying an investment. They're not, except in one small way. And, similarly, too many first-time investment property buyers let emotions get in the way of what is a money-making decision.

Homes

A home is where you live. When you're looking at homes for the first time, you want to be able to picture yourself living there and potentially creating happy memories. You should be able to see yourself in the home. There should be an emotional tug telling you 'this is the place'.

Homes should preferably be close to the various elements that make up your life. It should be roughly where you want to live, possibly near family and/or friends, near the kids' schools, or your work. It might be close to the cafes and restaurants you spend so much time at, or near great outdoor spaces that you crave after a week cooped up in an office.

Your home might have a yard for the kids or the dogs, or to put your two motorbikes, three cars and a boat. Or perhaps you specifically don't want any of that and you want an inner-city unit.

Your home needs to suit *your* lifestyle.

Do you really *need* to make money out of this property? No. That would be nice, but if all property prices stay flat for the next 50 years, it shouldn't really matter to you. You're in this place because it suits your lifestyle. (Even if this is a 'between' house and property prices don't rise, then your 'next' house isn't rising either.)

Homes don't get tax deductions for mortgage interest and there's no help paying the mortgage from tenants. But when you sell, there's also no capital gains tax (CGT) to pay.

Investment properties

Investment property is different. There should be only one reason for buying investment property. And that reason is …

…to make money.

People too often confuse the issue. A home is a place where you live and an investment property is about making money. In this case it does matter if property prices don't rise, because there are other options (shares, cash, bonds) you could be using to put your money to work.

It doesn't matter if you don't love the look of an investment property, that you couldn't imagine yourself living in that suburb, or that you think the house is too small for you. Why? Because you're never going to live there.

To buy an investment property, you need to divorce yourself from the sort of emotional logic that you use to buy a house. What sort of property gives you the most chance of making money, from both an income and a capital gains perspective?

Unlike a home, for this property, almost every cent you spend will become a tax deduction: the interest on the loan, the rates, the agent's fees, insurance costs and general maintenance.

It's all about the money. It's zero about emotion.

If it's not going to make financial sense, then it doesn't make any sense at all. Why would you spend hundreds of thousands of dollars on a place that you're not going to live in, if the primary aim wasn't to make money?

While it's a simple concept, many have great difficulty putting it into practice, particularly when buying a first investment property. The lack of emotion is important. Be a hard-arse!

Lining up the opposition

Sure, they're both made from a mixture of wood, brick, concrete, tiles, plasterboard, and so on. They could be identical in appearance and even be right next door to each other.

But if one of them is a home and one is an investment property, then their physical appearance is where the similarity ends.

In table 2.1, I lay out the main differences between homes and investment properties.

Table 2.1: homes versus investment properties

Question	Home	Investment property
Are you going to live there?	Yes	No
Does it need to be suitable to your lifestyle?	Yes, very important	No, not at all
Is it important that you can see yourself living in it?	Yes, very	No
Is it important that you like the feel of the house?	Yes—you need to feel comfortable	No
Is it important that you make money from it?	No, property prices don't need to move	Yes, or I would invest in something else
Will someone help you pay for it?	No	Yes (tenant and tax man)
Is interest tax-deductible?	No	Yes
Is there capital gains tax to pay?	No	Yes
Can you claim property costs against tax?	No	Yes
Do you get any ongoing tax breaks to subsidise the cost?	No	Yes
Is it likely to create wealth?	Yes	Yes

Can you see what I'm getting at? In most respects, an investment property and a home are different. One needs to meet personal needs. But financial reasons are what make an investment property stack up or not.

It's because of this that *Mortgages Made Easy* will occasionally be separated into streams. You might want to buy a home. Or you might be reading for investment property knowledge. And you might be here for knowledge on both.

Both types of property can create wealth

In the last question in table 2.1, we get a similarity. It's true that both types of property are *likely* to increase in value over the long term.

However, the sort of wealth each creates will be very, very different.

Let's take two identical houses next door to each other, with one owned by a homeowner and one by an investor. How would their fortunes differ? The homeowner will benefit over time from the house appreciating in value, as well as the home loan being paid down. That's how equity will be created. When the loan is finally paid off, the homeowner will have only a small cost in keeping the home going (unlike renters, who will be paying rent forever).

The investor will also benefit from the price of the property increasing and from the home loan being paid down (if they choose to do so). But they will also benefit from an income stream (rent) that will grow over time. Tax breaks will also be useful, until such time as the property is positively geared and tax is paid on the net income received.

When it comes to sale time, the homebuyer holds all the aces if a profit has been made. There is no capital gains tax to be paid on a *principal place of residence* (PPOR) when sold, no matter if the property has increased in value by $2 million.

If the investor sells and makes a profit, they have to pay capital gains tax (CGT) on the profit they make.

Home—the cornerstone of wealth creation

Given the differences between homes and investment properties, it is important to understand that a home plays an often critical part in most Australians' long-term wealth-creation strategies.

In fact, the family home will be *the cornerstone of wealth creation* for most Australians.

At the time most Australians retire, their home is likely to be their largest asset (the second largest will usually be superannuation).

But that's just a part of it. Homes also give you the opportunity to create further wealth, often by using the equity developed over time as *security* to purchase other investment assets. As I will show you in later chapters, your home can be a powerful source of equity to, for instance, purchase further property assets (and/or shares).

'I wouldn't risk the equity in my home for an investment!'

Sure. I understand, and that's perfectly understandable. Borrowing against your home to make other investments is adding a considerable risk to your finances. Taking higher risks to achieve potentially better outcomes will appeal to some and not to others.

But anyone who is borrowing money—whether to buy a home or an investment property—is taking on a greater financial risk in the short and medium terms than someone who doesn't borrow. This book is about debt; debt used to buy property. And sometimes, for those people who start out in property buying their own home, something will click about the whole property thing. And they will want to move into property investment also. This book will cover those options too.

I wanna piece of it!

Yeah, I know you do. And, believe me, I'm here to help. We're getting there. 'Patience, young Grasshopper.'

Given the underlying demand for land, wouldn't it be awesome if you could own a bit of it? And, a decade down the track, it's worth double what you paid for it? Well, that's essentially what can happen with a lot of property. As workers' incomes rise, as cities grow, as a greater number of people chase the same amount of land ... the prices paid for that land go up.

Getting a piece of the 'Great Australian Dream' is a serious business. For those buying a home, this is probably going to be the biggest purchase you're ever going to make.

For those buying their first investment property, it's a similar deal. The land that your property sits on is where the demand is.

Where does property wealth come from? Two sources. The first comes as the asset increases in value (see figure 2.1, overleaf). The second is an associated income stream coming from the asset (see figure 2.2, p. 19). When it comes to property, there's an added factor. And that's in regards to the debt decreasing.

Figure 2.1: how property creates wealth—homebuyers

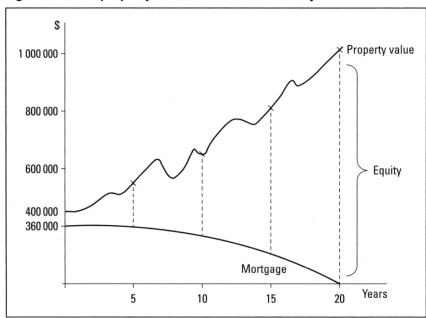

In figure 2.1, let's assume homebuyers have purchased our property. The value of our property rises by (let's say) 5 per cent a year. Property prices never move smoothly—they can rise and fall sharply—but that sort of growth is achievable over time.

Over that 20-year period, the value of the homebuyers' home increases from $400 000 to about $1 000 000 (actually $1 060 000, but let's not quibble over $60 000, hey). So, the house has grown in value by $600 000. But over the same period of time, the home loan has been paid down from $360 000 to $0. (While most mortgages are for 25 or 30 years, most are paid off well before that.)

The owners of this property are now sitting on an asset worth $1 million with no debt. Pretty cool, huh? That's not the end of the good news for homebuyers. But I'll come back to that.

Let's take the same equation for investors. Again, the property is purchased for $400 000 with a $360 000 debt. Again, with 5 per cent property appreciation, the property rises in value to $1 000 000.

Figure 2.2: how property creates wealth—investors

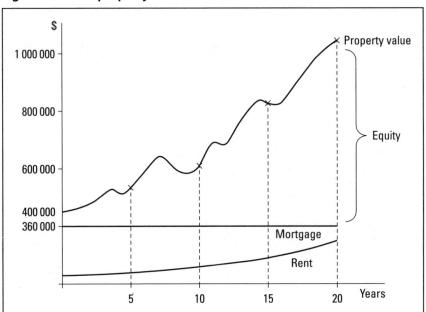

But, for tax reasons that are appropriate for some (and will be explained in chapter 6), the investors haven't paid off the debt, which remains at $360 000. The investors have still increased their wealth from an initial $40 000 to $640 000. (The capital not used to pay down debt could be used for other wealth creation plans, such as paying down their own home loan, or purchasing further investment properties.)

For the investors, another beautiful thing has happened. Over the holding period of 20 years, the rent that they were receiving has increased from $16 000 a year when they bought it (4 per cent of purchase price) to $40 000 a year (4 per cent of current value). That is, the income stream has also increased by 150 per cent.

Does it sound like the homebuyer is missing part of the deal here? The income stream?

Well, yes and no. Mr and Mrs Homebuyer aren't earning rent from their home. But now that they own their home, they're not having to pay to live in it. When they make their final loan repayment, the cost of living in their home falls considerably compared to what a renter would pay—to little more than rates, insurance and upkeep of the property. The next-door neighbours, who decided to rent instead of buy, are now paying $40 000 a year to live in their home—and this amount will continue to rise forever.

Property's main advantages can be summed up as follows. Property is an asset that:

- tends to rise strongly over time
- banks love to lend against
- either:
  - provides a rising income stream (investors), or
  - provides a long-term, low-cost roof over your head (homeowners).

Harnessing the power

That, in essence, is the power of property ownership. Outside of some higher-risk strategies, such as property development, flipping or renovations, *property uses time to create wealth*.

Simply, real estate is not a get-rich-quick scheme. Run away from anyone, or any thing, such as an advertisement, that tries to suggest otherwise.

No matter what a suave property spruiker might claim at one of their overpriced (or even free) seminars—which are, all too often, selling properties developed by related parties—property takes time to create wealth. Good property can do the wealth-creation job *beautifully*, but it's not like doing a six-week course to learn Spanish before travelling to South America.

Sadly, the property industry is filled with high-profile snake-oil salesmen, who claim getting rich via property is a cinch. That's bollocks. It can't be done—not without taking some extraordinary risks. A buy-and-hold strategy is the safest, least risky and most reliable way to create property wealth. Property's power, based on you buying properly, should really start to show itself between about the five- and ten-year mark, but will prove best if done over decades.

A bit of pain never hurt…

And owning property is rarely painless. Property almost inevitably has some financial discomfort associated with it.

Buying a property—to live or to invest in—usually comes with financial sacrifice. For example, it is almost always cheaper in the short *and* medium terms to rent a house, rather than buy it.

But with all property, if you're tipping money in, either by way of a deposit or ongoing financial contributions via negative gearing, you are not able to spend that money in other ways now.

At its worst, bad property can be a financial disaster. It can send you more broke than *Two Broke Girls*. All the way to bankruptcy. Not all property will increase in value over time. Property can go backwards—even good property—for extended periods. Some property can fall in value by half, or worse, *plus* become a massive drain on your cashflow.

Spruikers—the perfect storm for a property disaster

Certainly, the primary driver of the success of a property is the property itself. But this book places a bigger focus on making sure you get the other major factors that can impact on a property's success right.

These are financing, and structuring your loans to suit the aim of your property purchase.

A perfect storm for wealth destruction can happen in a number of ways. Often it's because people don't understand enough about the complex investment that property is and they try to do it themselves.

Sadly, where I see it happen most is when investors get sucked into the 'Property Spruiker Abyss'. I get it; they're slick, and their tales of untold wealth seem compelling. However, what you are typically being funnelled into is a high-pressure sales and marketing drive for what is too often a property developer, or a business that will be rewarded by a developer. Sometimes the developer is also picking up a slice of your finance pie, by selling the loan.

Not all those who stand on a stage to talk property are spruikers who should be avoided. But the risk of serious conflicts of interest rise exponentially, in my opinion, where the investor would be buying a property being developed by the person giving the advice, or where the person giving the advice will be receiving payments from a developer. (It is for this reason that Bruce Brammall Financial has never dealt with developers. We use fee-for-service property advocates to purchase existing properties for clients.)

Stepping over the landmines — avoiding the duds

What makes a bad property investment? Plenty of things, many of which are easy enough to spot, if you've had some time in the property game — and I'll be sharing some of those tips throughout this book.

I have eight rules for buying investment property. I've always used these rules personally, and also to assist Bruce Brammall Financial's clients when purchasing property through carefully selected buyer's advocates. These rules are about location, land value, cashflow and who you're buying from (for example, we would *never* buy from property developers).

My rules are as much about what we won't buy for clients. They are designed to stop clients from buying property that is obviously wrong, which can be more than half the battle. Avoiding bad property makes it so much easier to get in the top half of property performers.

Property and debt — the critical understanding

Who has $650 000 sitting in a bank account ready to purchase the *average* home in Australia? Very few. But all property is owned by someone, and new buyers replace old owners all the time.

How do they buy property if they don't have the money in their bank account? With debt, of course. The vast majority of property purchased in Australia is completed with the help of debt.

Debt allows you to buy something now that you couldn't otherwise afford. This includes homes. Without stupendously big gifts or bequests from parents or grandparents, no first-home buyer can afford to buy their home outright. And buying a home is one of debt's great uses.

Some debt is truly awful for your finances, like credit cards that aren't paid off in full each month and car loans where you're encouraged to spend more on the car than you would have otherwise because the finance is so easy. (Why do most car dealerships have their own finance teams on site?)

But you are probably hoping to access debt for one of two great purposes. The first, to buy a home, is about providing security for your family. The second, to buy investment properties, is about creating wealth. Debt done properly can be a fantastic partner that will help you grow your wealth.

Why? Because it allows you to buy something now that will (generally) appreciate over time; go back and check over figures 2.1 and 2.2 (on p. 18 and p. 19 respectively) again. But getting that debt right is critical.

Property success—the three ingredients

Broadly, there are three critical ingredients when it comes to making a success of property.

They are:

1   buying the right property

2   using a suitable debt structure

3   getting the ownership right.

One unarguable truth about property is that *you make your money when you buy*. The better the deal when you purchase, the more profitable it will be. Many think that you can just buy the right property and everything will be okay. If you buy an awesome property (and millions of properties can be awesome at the right price), then most of your return will be looked after by the property itself.

But you can't just focus on the property. If you want cream and cherries on your property's performance, you'll need to ensure your structures are right, both for finance and ownership.

Property is so much about the associated debt. Bugger up the structuring of either the debt or the ownership (which you need to get right up front) and you can turn a good property purchase bad very quickly. Get it right and it can add superior returns to your investment.

Property is a big, lumpy asset class. Most other investments you can buy in small chunks and, similarly, add to in small chunks. But property comes in minimums of a few hundred thousand dollars. When you make a mistake on something that costs a few hundred thousand dollars, it's going to be more than pocket change to fix it, if it can be fixed at all. We'll give you some examples of how getting things wrong can cost you tens of thousands of dollars in chapters 5 through 7.

So, let's not delay this any longer. Let's start getting mortgage fit.

Property purchasing principles

I struggled for a long time with the following concept: 'If property is that good and that sure of making money, why doesn't everyone just do it?'

There are plenty of reasons. But the most important one is that so many people lose so much money on property by getting bad advice, or by purchasing property that was always going to cause them headaches. And there is one way that people lose more money than any other.

There are many great property experts and advocates out there. If you're a good learner, you'll pick up one to ten tips from each of them. But if you get nothing else out of this book, the following tip could pay for this book a thousand times over.

If the person on the stage is recommending you purchase a particular brand-new (development) property and they have an interest in the company that is selling that property ... walk away. They are not interested in your financial wellbeing—they are only interested in selling their latest development property for the maximum profit they can. Learn whatever you can from them and use that knowledge to purchase somewhere else.

And just to ram it home ... here are the key points to take away from this chapter.

- Property can be a great investment because demand will always be high.

- The power of property comes from the scarcity of land.

- Homes are not primarily investments and do not need to make money.

- Investment properties are all about making money and zero about emotion.

- Both homes and investment properties can create wealth.

- Home ownership is the cornerstone of wealth creation in Australia; and debt is necessary in home ownership.

- Property wealth comes from increases in your asset value and from associated income streams (rent).

- Property uses time to create wealth.

- Property spruikers should be avoided at all costs.

- Debt is necessary to invest in property.

- There are three key ingredients to property success: buying the right property; using a suitable debt structure; and getting the ownership right.

3

Getting mortgage fit

You're right to dive into this property caper, are you? Property is pushing your buttons. The dream has been brewing in the back of your mind for a while. And nothing you've read here so far has made you waver at all.

You've decided on a home or investment property. Short of winning the lotto, you understand this is going to involve borrowing huge wads of cash. Now you want directions to the starting line.

Right, next … are you financially fit? Do you know what I'm talking about? Could you flex your financial biceps and have a mortgage broker fawn over you, like John Travolta when Olivia Newton-John began belting out 'You're the One That I Want' in *Grease*? If you truly are financially fit, banks will fall over themselves to show you the money.

Some people are naturally financially fit. Others are carrying a few extra pounds. Some could spend a year working hard on becoming a 'Financial Biggest Loser' and still come up short. Fixing your finances can be harder than dropping 10 kilos.

So, for the next little while, you're going to imagine that I'm the Michelle Bridges of your personal finances. And, if you're not scoring a big tick for these things, you're going to 'just do it', okay? This is going to require a diet high in delayed gratification, low in credit card calories, with plenty of cost-cutting exercises.

If you don't, you'll be eliminating yourself from the property game. And while that stinks, you'll know who to blame.

Saving a deposit

Saving a deposit is a bit like sands through the hourglass. It's made up of thousands of little things (dollars) that need to flow into the right place (your bank account).

There's only one way to do that: save your butt off.

The good news is that once you really set your mind to it, it probably won't take as long as you think (and some budgeting tough love is coming up next). I've asked a lot of people how long it took them, as an individual or a couple, to save enough money to buy. And the average, once they made the decision, is 12 to 18 months. Surprisingly, few take longer than two years.

First Home Saver accounts—a warning

Politicians blither and blather about 'affordability' and want to be seen to be doing something for first-home buyers. Rarely do they do much. And thankfully so—the one thing that is almost certain in a market for anything, is that if it is no longer affordable, then people will stop buying it. Housing is no different. Economics 101.

Sadly, though, the blithering sometimes produces action.

To this end, in 2008 we got First Home Saver Accounts. Essentially, the government gave you a savings bonus for putting money away to buy a home, and a lower taxation rate on the earnings in that account. The earliest version actually locked you out of the market for four years, which was demonstrably stupid and they removed that rule after a few years.

The latest concern is a plan to allow first-home buyers to access up to $25 000 of their super to buy a home, and then pay that money back into super over 15 years. First-home buyers, you do not want this plan to eventuate. Pouring extra money into the system will cause prices to spike. Nothing surer. And, therefore, you would simply be robbing your future to buy an overpriced house now. Hopefully this thought bubble gets pricked, for the sake of first-home buyers.

Saving a deposit requires setting yourself a goal. How much will you need for your own deposit? Start working methodically towards that. It will involve some sacrifice. It might require you to actually set yourself a budget (blech!).

The myth of the 10 per cent deposit

People talk about having a 10 per cent deposit when buying a property—whether that's a home or an investment. But that's a furphy that creates serious misconceptions.

If you want to buy a house for $500 000, how much would a 10 per cent deposit be? $50 000? That would leave you with a loan for $450 000, right? Wrong.

You're forgetting stamp duty. And potentially lenders' mortgage insurance (LMI), and a few other expensive incidentals. Stamp duty can be up to about 5.5 per cent, depending on which state you live in and whether you're buying a home or an investment property. Stamp duty is charged by state and territory governments. It's an expensive, wretched tax, for which you get nothing. (See later in this chapter for more on stamp duty.)

So when they talk about a 10 per cent deposit, it usually really means about 15 per cent. Let's take the example above, for a $500 000 house. If you had $75 000, or 15 per cent, you would lose about $25 000 to stamp duty and other fees, and have approximately $50 000 as a 10 per cent deposit for a house, leaving a loan of approximately $450 000, or 90 per cent of the purchase price.

Also be aware that when you borrow more than 80 per cent of the purchase price, you will be required to pay lenders' mortgage insurance (LMI). See chapter 7 for more on LMI.

Banging a budget into shape

You: 'Hey, do we really have to deal with boring rubbish like budgets?'

Me: 'Yup. Sorry. Though, some of you can skip this bit.'

If you've got plenty of savings—that is, tens of thousands of dollars or more—and every week or month you add to your stash, you can skip this bit and move on.

Good savers might never have done a budget, because they have an instinctive feel for how much is coming in and how much is going out. When they're feeling like there's not much coming in, a little electrical pulse shoots through to their brain and they rein in the spending to match the income gap. They understand the difference between needs and wants and weight spending to the former rather than the latter.

If that's not you—and the stats suggest it probably isn't—continue reading.

You cannot buy your first property without a deposit. In order to get a deposit, you need to save. If you can't save, you need a budget to help you. If you can't be bothered developing a budget to get you to that first goal, then you've wasted your money on this book.

Only non-mainstream lenders and some interests associated with property developers—neither of which should you be aiming for as your preferred lenders—will lend you money if you can't save a deposit. Fringe lenders can be painful, with higher interest rates and poor service levels.

Free download—budgeting tool

For a free budgeting tool, go to www.brucebrammallfinancial.com.au and put *budget template* into the search engine.

This free budget template is a reasonably comprehensive tool that will allow you to enter, by month, your income and your major expenses. As it is an Excel spreadsheet, it will add up along the right and across the bottom.

This will help you track and plan for your big regular expenses, including insurances (car, contents, health, and so on) average monthly spending on groceries, entertainment, rent, mortgage, utilities, and so on. You will need something like a notepad and pen to tally the small expenses (coffees, magazines, lunches, drinks at the pub, gifts, and so on) that pile up every day.

If you haven't been able to save to this point, I'm sorry, but budgeting is probably your best option. To buy property, you should be aiming for approximately at least 15 per cent of the purchase price, 5 per cent of which will go towards stamp duty. See chapter 5 for more on this.

Putting on a 'bag of fruit'

Back before the early 1990s, if you wanted a loan, you had to make an appointment with your bank manager, put on your bag of fruit (suit) and polish up on your Queen's English.

Nowadays, what you're wearing matters not. For all they care, you could have dreadlocks, sleeves of tattoos running up and down your arms and legs, have 15 body parts pierced and be wearing a 'Satan rocks' T-shirt. They won't even know, because in this age of mortgage brokers, email and internet commerce, there's a good chance nobody from the bank will ever meet you.

But, figuratively, you need to put on your financial bag of fruit. And that means getting your finances into such shape that they'll take one look at you and just see 'a beautiful set of numbers'.

Get your free credit report

If you're going for your first property loan, or your first one in a while, and you're not quite sure how your credit record is looking, start by finding out what lenders are going to instantly find out about you.

There are two main credit agencies in Australia—Veda Advantage and Dun & Bradstreet. By law, these two organisations must provide you free access to your credit report. They both have two services. You can pay (about $50 to $70) to get your credit report within 24 hours. Or you can order the free version, which will take about ten days to be sent to you.

If you go through their websites (www.mycreditfile.com.au for Veda Advantage and www.dnb.com.au for Dun & Bradstreet), search for *free credit report*.

If you haven't done this before, your credit report might come as a bit of a shock. Problems with phone providers, utility bill payments, bank loans and tax bills can often spring up here.

If there are mistakes on there, or reports that were resolved but haven't been corrected, you will need to contact the institution immediately and request that they fix it on the report—they have a responsibility to fix errors.

Credit cards — a blade with two sharp edges

When it comes to credit cards, there are two types of people on this earth — transactors and revolvers.

Transactors buy everything on their credit card, but pay it off in full at the end of every month. Revolvers rarely pay off their debt in full and roll the debt over each month. As a result, they pay interest on their credit card balances on an ongoing basis. Banks love revolvers. And transactors love revolvers. Revolvers, in essence, pay for the reward points for transactors (who pay nothing really) and also for the banks to make healthy profits.

Having overblown credit card debts is seriously bad for your financial health. If you've got multiple cards and high credit limits that are never paid off, not only are you paying interest rates that are usually 12 to 20 per cent, but you are also severely limiting how much you can borrow to buy property.

And when it comes to buying property, credit cards are even more evil. When calculating what you can afford to pay, lenders will *always assume that your credit cards are maxed out*. That is, if you have a limit of $20 000, they assume that you have spent the whole $20 000 and need to repay this at 2.5 to 3 per cent a month (or $7200 a year in this case) — even if you have always paid off your credit cards in full each month.

Why? Because you *could* rack up debt on your credit card if you needed to. So banks assume the worst. That payment can markedly reduce the amount of money you can borrow.

The real cost of credit cards to property buyers

Let's take two women earning $80 000 a year. One has a credit card limit of $5000, while the other has a $20 000 limit. All other details will be the same.

Comparing the same lender, the woman with the $5000 credit limit could borrow $552 000, while the one with the higher card limit could only borrow $498 000. Even if neither of them ever uses their credit cards, the woman with the higher credit card limit has had her borrowing limit reduced by $54 000.

Put another way, every $1 higher on the credit limit has reduced her borrowing capacity by $3.60. However, every lender has different rules.

If you have massive credit card limits that you don't need and never use, reduce them. (In some instances, it can make the difference in getting a loan approved.)

Cleaning up your credit record

Santa knew whether you'd been bad or good. He just knew. The fear of getting into his bad books was enough to keep you on the straight and narrow ... at least through December.

Banks also know whether you've been bad or good. And, simply, because so many people want so much money from them, they don't have to deal with the bad ones if they don't want to. The big banks can pick and choose their customers.

A good credit record is crucial to property investment. You can't buy property without debt. And the people who control approval of that debt aren't dummies. Banks don't get many failed loans. In early 2014, approximately 0.45 per cent of loans were 'in arrears 90 days or more'. Less than one in 200 customers had got into debt trouble. (And arrears of 90 days or more doesn't guarantee those borrowers will fail on their loans.)

Banks know how to assess the likelihood that you'll get into trouble. From a quick look at your bank statements and credit cards, your previous mortgages and your record of paying bills, they can make reasonably accurate predictions.

If you want to access the best rates at the most reputable banks, you need a clean credit record. If your credit rating isn't shining so brightly, you might still be able to get a loan to buy a property, but not at the best rates or conditions. Higher interest rates reduce the returns for investors, and make it harder for first-home buyers to own their home sooner.

Also, in March 2014, Australia's privacy laws changed to make the job of keeping a clean credit record a little trickier. In came what's known as *positive credit reporting*. In the past, companies only reported to agencies if you'd been really bad — epic fails in meeting financial agreements. The new *positive* reporting meant that those agencies will now know when you've been a little bit bad too. The upside is that your good habits will also be reported.

Good work history

It should go without saying that when a bank is lending you hundreds of thousands of dollars, they want to know that you can hold down a job.

Further, they want *stability* in your income and work history. Whether you are an employee or self-employed, working full-time or part-time, banks want to know that you have a stable (or rising) income. They will usually ask for three years' worth of work history.

The self-employed have separate issues, as income is rarely stable. Their income might rise and fall and rise again over a three-year period. If this is the case, banks will often want to base the amount they lend to you on the worst of the last two years' income. Some banks only want one year's income figures (which might include profit and loss statements, income tax returns and notices of assessment). The self-employed will generally benefit more from using a mortgage broker, as brokers know individual banks' policies and will quickly be able to find banks that are more friendly to the ups and downs of the incomes of the self-employed.

Savings history—5 per cent genuine savings

This should also be obvious—banks won't lend to people who have never shown any ability to save money.

Particularly for first-home buyers, banks will usually insist on *5 per cent genuine savings*. You will need to show records of your savings account (usually three months, but sometimes six months). They often downplay 'gifts' from family members and will often discount those gifts completely until they have been in your account for three months without being spent.

Understanding the different types of debt

Debt comes in different types. It's not all evil. Some of it is pretty good—particularly the sort that allows you to purchase property, obviously.

The media is filled with the concept of *good* and *bad* debt, where the difference between the two is determined only by whether or not it gets a tax deduction (good debt gets the deduction).

That's unfair to debt, because that means a home loan is bad debt. Is getting a loan and buying a home for the future of you and your family *bad*? Not in my opinion.

I believe there are three types of debt. As I outlined in *Debt Man Walking*, the three types of debt are the *D.O.G.* of debt—dumb, okay and great.

There are two questions to ask about a debt:

1   Is the interest on the debt tax-deductible?

2   Is the asset purchased likely to increase in value?

Dumb debt answers no to both questions—it's neither a tax deduction, nor used to purchase items that are likely to increase in value. That means pretty much anything bought on a credit card—most cars, furniture, personal loans and so on—would be classified as dumb debt.

Okay debt answers yes to one of those questions. Either the interest on the debt is a tax deduction, or the asset purchased is likely to increase in value. That puts homes and work cars into the *okay* debt category, along with computers that classify as tax deductions.

Great debt sits out on its own. The interest on the debt of the asset that you've purchased qualifies as a tax deduction and the asset is likely to increase in value. That includes the likes of investment properties and other investments, such as shares, or ownership in companies.

The joy of deductible debt

I know $1 million seems like a lot of debt ... but those with a family home and even just one investment property are often going to have this amount. (And those looking to build bigger property investment portfolios might have to get used to having debt in the millions of dollars.)

Tax deductions and debt are important. If the interest qualifies for a tax deduction, it will be far cheaper to service the debt. For the tax man, debt on an investment that is producing income will usually qualify as deductible debt.

If you have $1 million worth of debt on your home and interest rates are at 6.5 per cent, then the cost of servicing that debt (interest-only) will be $65 000 if there is no tax deduction involved.

If the debt is for an income-producing asset (such as property), an interest rate of 6.5 per cent will still lead to interest of $65 000 being paid. However, as the interest is tax-deductible, the borrower will get a tax deduction for interest paid.

If the borrower is on the highest marginal tax rate (earning more than $180 000 in FY15), they would get back 49 per cent of the $65 000, reducing the net cost of the debt from $65 000 to $33 150, after a tax deduction of $31 850.

For those earning $80 000 to $180 000, the marginal tax rate is 39 per cent. On interest of $65 000, a tax return of $25 350 would be received, reducing the net cost to $39 650.

And on the *average* marginal tax rate of 34.5 per cent, the cost of the $65 000 interest debt would reduce to $42 575 after a tax return of $22 425.

(These examples do not include the impact of income paid on the investments.)

Paying down dumb debt

If you have dumb debt — for credit cards, personal loans and car loans in particular — concentrating on paying off this debt can add substantially to your ability to borrow.

Dumb debt usually comes with high interest rates. If you're paying higher interest rates on this sort of debt, banks are simply going to be a little more cautious about you. You will usually be better off using savings to pay down this debt — it will save you more interest than you'll earn on your savings.

What banks want — getting your paperwork in order

Banks aren't dummies. Sure, sometimes they might make themselves look stupid, such as when they went too far in sacking staff and closing branches in the 1990s — a time when bank-bashing almost replaced cricket as the national sport in Australia.

Bank systems are pretty tight. Even at the height of the Global Financial Crisis in 2008–09, the number of borrowers who got into trouble stayed below 0.7 per cent of all customers in Australia.

Banks do their research up front. They will crawl around in your financial intestines, trying to find out your financial weaknesses. If you've got one, or have had financial difficulties in the past, there's a very good chance the banks will find out about it, partly through the credit checks they run and what they can see in the bank statements you must show them.

Whether you apply to banks yourself, or use a mortgage broker, the type of information you're going to need will be similar. But brokers have contacts and know bank lending policies.

Banks don't all take the same risks. Some lenders are good with small business owners, some banks restrict lending in certain postcodes, some prefer certain professionals, some restrict by building type ... you won't believe some of the rules lenders set. But you also won't know. And there's a far better chance a good mortgage broker will know one from the next. See later in this chapter for more on mortgage brokers.

What info will the banks want?

Plenty. The more complex your financial situation, the more detail they'll be after. In some cases, I've filed hundreds of pages of documents for relatively small loans ... and every single page was needed, or the loan wouldn't have been approved.

Everybody's situation is a little different. But the following list is what the vast majority of banks are going to ask for.

- *Proof of identity*. Usually driver's licences, but they might also request passports, marriage certificates and citizenship certificates to meet identification or residency requirements.

- *Income verification information*.
  - Employees: Between one and three pay slips with year-to-date salary figures on them, potentially PAYG summaries, employment contracts and even bank statements to prove salary deposits. Bonuses might not be accepted without some history of payments.

- – Self-employed: Most banks will want two full years of profit and loss statements and tax returns from the companies or trusts. If there are multiple companies and trusts, they will want to see the lot. Plus your own personal tax returns.

- *Details of other income received.* Including government assistance, managed fund distributions or share dividends.

- *Your existing bank, credit and savings accounts.*

  - – Savings accounts: They will want to see three to six months of savings account history. For first-home buyers with small deposits, banks will want to see the minimum *genuine 5 per cent savings* (see earlier in this chapter).

  - – Credit cards: Three months' worth of full credit card statements for every credit card. Many banks will go through the spending on them line by line and may come back with curly questions on your spending patterns.

  - – Personal loans: Generally three months' worth of full statements for personal loans for everything you might will owe money on.

  - – Existing property loans: Nothing is more sacred to banks regarding a prospective customer than the performance on their existing property loans. They will want to see, for all property loans, six months' worth of bank statements.

These details will generally be required for everyone. However, if you're a property investor or homeowner, they will also want to see current lease agreements, rent statements and/or rates notices.

Every bank has different requirements. But what all banks are trying to do is find out that you've been a good customer and that you pay your loans, debts and bills on time. If they see that you occasionally get charged late fees or fines, or penalty interest, it will raise red flags for them. Plenty of people want the bank's money, and the bank would rather lend it to someone who is a better credit risk.

Self-employed—ain't it hard enough?

With an increasingly flexible workforce, more and more people are either self-employed, on contract, or have odd working conditions. Banks are conservative. And they don't like uncertainty. But they are getting better with being understanding of these issues.

The self-employed face the most consistent hurdles and will usually have to present the most paperwork (which can mostly be done electronically nowadays). Returns from companies and trusts (all of them) will usually be required. Just be aware that the bank, possibly via your broker, might come back with multiple requests for information. It can be a bit of a process. Don't get disheartened, but also understand a good broker will be worth their weight in gold here.

Odd bank rules—an introduction

Naturally, some banks are bound to be bigger bastards than others! Aah, cheap shot. Sorry. But my point is that not all banks are the same. Some of them don't want to take certain risks.

Some have very, very unusual rules when it comes to what they will and won't lend against. And these rules can make huge differences to how much you can borrow. Indeed, they can be the difference between being able to borrow and not being able to borrow.

A few brief examples:

- For a fully paid company car, one lender might add $0, while another will add $10 000 to your income, which can make a big difference when it comes to income for servicing your loan.

- For the self-employed, some lenders only want one year's worth of earnings. This can be helpful for relatively new small-business owners who don't have two years' worth of business history.

- If you have a new employer, some lenders will supply you a loan with your first pay slip, though most will want to see several and some might not want you until you're out of probation with that employer.

There are too many odd rules to list. But understand this: getting knocked back on one bank's policies can be very disheartening and can make you doubt whether you can get a loan. A good mortgage broker will know the policies of a variety of banks and will be able to find you a suitable lender first time around.

Getting pre-approval

If you're about to make the biggest purchase of your life (or even just another huge one, if you're making a second or subsequent property purchase), then you're going to want to know for certain that when you sign the contract, a bank will actually lend you the money, right?

You can know this. It's called a *pre-approval*, or an *approval in principle*. This is a bank saying that they've seen your finances up front and have agreed to lend you up to a certain amount of money.

You won't always need a pre-approval. If your finances are particularly strong—which your mortgage broker or bank might be able to give you some security about—then a pre-approval might not be necessary. (However, if you're buying an investment property with all debt, make sure you read about the importance of getting this area right in chapter 7.)

A pre-approval will be very important for people who might be borrowing close to their limits, as it allows them to bid with comfort on a property and to know what limit they can spend. There's no point bidding on a property up to $600000 if the bank has stated that the maximum that they will lend you will only cover a purchase of $550000.

Getting a pre-approval usually entails the full application process, up front. That is, they want to see *everything*, except the contract of sale (which you don't have yet): all financials, credit cards, pay slips and so on, as laid out earlier in this chapter.

While pre-approvals sound great, they're not foolproof. And the quality of pre-approvals varies from bank to bank. For example:

- Pre-approvals are normally granted for a specific time period—usually three or six months. Despite the pre-approval, banks will often ask for more information after you hand them the contract, such as updated pay slips.

- If you have bought a rental property, they might include conditions, such as a minimum required weekly rental.

- They will often depend on a *satisfactory bank valuation* of the property.

For the cautious, those buying their first home, or those who are borrowing close to their limits, a pre-approval can be important. While many banks might lend you enough money to be able to settle on your property, it is better to make sure up front that a bank will lend to you on acceptable terms than to try to deal with a bank when you're under time pressure to settle.

However, if you have a huge deposit, and you believe an assurance that you could borrow hundreds of thousands of dollars more than you would need, then a pre-approval might not be required.

Guarantors — security at a price

Sometimes, buyers need a helping hand. They can't quite get there on their own. They're a little short on the deposit or a little short on being able to meet the repayments.

The answer can be to have a *guarantor* assist you with the purchase. A guarantor (usually a family member, but it can technically be anyone) is agreeing to step in to make good on the loan in the event the customer defaults or is unable to pay. It is a very serious commitment and, increasingly, banks will insist on the family member getting independent legal advice before signing the document.

There are two types of guarantor — *security guarantors* and *servicing guarantors*.

A *security guarantor* usually puts up a portion of their own property as security to assist someone who has a small deposit. This can help them get enough security to get the loan and might remove the need to pay lender's mortgage insurance (LMI).

Here's an example. Let's say a young couple is buying a house worth $450 000. They have a deposit of $60 000, which is enough to cover $45 000 for the 10 per cent deposit plus stamp duty and other costs. However, they are going to be hit with a $9000 LMI bill, because they are borrowing more than 80 per cent of the value of the home. One of their parents, who owns their home outright, is prepared to go security guarantor for their child. In this instance, it would involve going guarantor for at least $45 000 against the parent's home, which would bring the loan back below 80 per cent.

A *servicing guarantor* is almost becoming a thing of the past now, with recent changes in laws. But traditionally a servicing guarantor would promise to step in with their income to assist repaying the debt if the borrowers got into difficulty. Governments decided this was causing too many problems, with banks having to act on these guarantees, so changed the rules to make it far more difficult for these guarantees to be offered. At the time of writing, most banks weren't offering them for individuals, but some were allowing companies to become a servicing guarantor.

Parents want to help, but try to leave them out of it

Parents: ah, bless 'em. Can we not let go of the apron strings? Or do they not want empty nest syndrome to kick in?

Many parents want to help their kids get into their first homes, which is lovely. Some will offer cash as a gift. Others might be willing to put their homes up as security to save on LMI.

Just be wary of putting your parents in harm's way. They've worked hard all their lives. They have less time to financially recover from any potential disaster than you do. Losing their home, or having to take out a mortgage on their home to cover you if you run into trouble ... it's not a position we want to put them in, is it?

In most cases, getting someone to go guarantor means that you simply haven't saved enough yet. Consider working on that savings thing a bit longer before drawing your parents into it.

Understanding stamp duty

Stamp duty! The bane of property buyers.

Stamp duty is a state-based regressive tax that is usually charged as a percentage of the purchase cost. It often adds tens of thousands of dollars to the cost of buying property. The person who pays the tax gets nothing directly for it (although it forms part of an investor's capital base and therefore they recoup a portion of the cost when they sell, *if* they sell).

But it has also become a little fairer in recent years. State governments now charge less stamp duty, or potentially none at all, to those who are buying a home, as compared with investment property buyers.

As a charge, it's all over the shop.

In Victoria, for instance, stamp duty for an investor on a $500000 established property is $25070. In Queensland, stamp duty for a property of the same value would be $15925.

For a first-home buyer, stamp duty on a $500000 home would be $0 in Queensland and WA, while it would be as much as $21330 for a South Australian.

And there are myriad other unique state-based rules. For example, Victoria gives stamp duty concessions to off-the-plan properties, as an incentive to buy new property and to stimulate the building industry. That is, if the home hasn't been completed, you only pay the portion of the stamp duty that equates to how complete the building is. If it's just vacant land, there might not be much stamp duty to pay. If the building is half completed, you will have to pay proportionately more.

Also unusually, stamp duty in the ACT is a tax deduction against income for property investors.

For more information on stamp duty in your state (and because the rates seem to change in at least one or two states each year), search for *stamp duty calculator* in a search engine, or at www.brucebrammallfinancial. com.au, to determine the duty for your intended purchase. This is the biggest cost for a property—and, sadly, one that cannot be avoided.

First Home Owner's Grant

The First Home Owner's Grant (FHOG) was introduced in 2000 to help offset the cost of the then-new GST. Initially, it was a national scheme. Now administered by state and territory governments, the scheme has splintered and different bonuses are offered everywhere.

Money or incentives might be offered to buy new homes, or homes under certain values, or homes in rural or regional locations. This offer varies state by state. If you are purchasing your first home, go to the federal government's website, www.firsthome.gov.au, which will provide you with links to get to your own state's FHOG offers and incentives, or search for the calculators at www.brucebrammallfinancial.com.au.

More costs of purchasing

The costs of purchase don't end with stamp duty. The other fees that you are likely to incur when you purchase a property include:

- *Conveyancing fees.* Usually $600 to $1200 for an average property, paid to a specialist conveyancer or solicitor to assist with the legal transfer of title to you.

- *Loan fees.* With most banks, this is usually no more than $600 and is often discounted, or not charged at all.

- *Mortgage registration fees.* These fees usually run from $100 to $300 when the mortgage is registered by the bank with a state government.

- *Valuation fees.* These can be several hundred dollars, but they are often absorbed by the lender.

- *Title searches.* This cost is often included in the conveyancer's fees.

DIY or mortgage broker?

When it comes to finding the right lender for your situation, there are three main options:

1 Go to your existing bank.

2 Do-it-yourself with the research and application process.

3 Use a mortgage broker.

If you're getting your first loan, going to your existing bank is unlikely to be your best option. With the thousands of lending products out there, what are the chances that your bank will have the most suitable loan for your circumstances, both for rates and any additional services you might want? Minuscule.

But if you are keen on your current bank, here's how you can make that work. At a minimum, do some reasonable research yourself first. Then challenge your bank to match the best you've found.

Next is the DIY option, starting with a clean slate. You need to be a good researcher and potentially a good negotiator. Doing it yourself can be personally rewarding, like any DIY project can. If you're a fast learner and a natural researcher, this could be the option for you. In chapter 4, I go into detail on loan products themselves, so that you can compare one lender's products to the next.

This can also be a good option if interest rates are your most important consideration. Once you've sized up the sort of loan you want, then you might enjoy strong-arming a few banks to get yourself the best deal or package.

There are good websites that you can use as a starting point for your research, including www.cannex.com.au and www.infochoice.com.au (plus you'll find plenty of up-to-date information, commentary and calculators at www.brucebrammallfinancial.com.au). Some sites will give you great information on rates and what bells and whistles each product has.

The onus will, of course, be on you to make sure you've done your research correctly. If you're up for the challenge (and it certainly can be a challenge!), then chapter 4 gives you a starting point for finding out what you need to know.

For everyone else, getting a mortgage is likely to be something that you only do once or twice in a lifetime. Educating yourself about the finer points of a loan might be a mountain you have no interest in climbing. Or you might not have the time.

Mortgage brokers will, undoubtedly, save you potentially dozens of hours of time, and probably money. They will teach you the basics of the various mortgage products, help make the final decision as to which lender might work best for you, then negotiate with them, help fill out their forms and conduct all of the follow-ups until the loan is approved.

For things I'm never going to be an expert in, I use professionals. My specialties are mortgage broking, financial planning and writing. When it comes to law, accounting, medicine... I'm happy to pay others for their knowledge. I don't have the time. Professionals get it right first time, saving me untold hours of research. They give me more time with my kids and doing those things that I want to do, such as build my businesses.

If that's also you, get a mortgage broker on your team. Good brokers will have dozens of lenders on their 'panel' to choose from, potentially covering hundreds of different types of loans. They know which banks are doing deals (banks are competitive and offer discounts that change regularly) and which products that each bank offers will suit your situation.

More importantly, they will know *bank policy*. Individual banks have policies that outline who they will and won't lend to, under what circumstances, in which postcodes, at what loan-to-valuation ratio (LVR), with which allowances and at what rate. These really important details are not available on websites. If there's anything other than plain vanilla (that is, you're an employee, with considerable savings, buying in a 'safe' suburb) in your application, then you often won't find out that a bank doesn't deal with your situation until after you put in your application.

And, to top it off, policy can change at a moment's notice.

If the mortgage broker doesn't know the policies off the top of their heads, they will have the contacts to quickly be able to find out specific policy and compare that policy with other lenders.

Commissions — how brokers are paid

Of course, mortgage brokers are paid. The way the industry is currently set up, that is generally by commission. A commission is a payment that is built into a product. In the case of mortgage broking, the payment is made from the lender to the broker.

It usually comes at no direct cost to the consumer. That is, banks either have to pay their own people to source and package the loans to consumers, or they can pay 'introducers' (brokers) to do that for them.

Some people believe banks will offer you cheaper rates if you go direct. This is incorrect. Brokers are often able to get better rates from banks than bank staff are, because of their ability to negotiate. Where else can a bank employee go if they don't like their own bank's deal for a client?

Commissions for residential property loans in Australia tend to be twofold. There are up-front commissions to write the loan (on average, about 0.6-0.7 per cent). And there are ongoing trails, which tend to be between 0.15 per cent and 0.4 per cent, depending on the lender.

Commissions and conflicts of interest

One of the main potential problems with commissions (in any commission-driven industry) is the potential for conflicts of interest. If one lender offers a higher commission than another, then is a broker more likely to recommend that loan?

Potentially, yes. However, the offers from most lenders tend to be fairly similar. If they do have a lower up-front commission, then they tend to have a higher ongoing commission, and vice versa. While commissions are charged, this potential for conflict of interest will remain.

If you are concerned about the lender your broker has recommended, ask them to explain how the commission differs between the chosen bank and another bank or two of your choice.

Property purchasing principles

Safe as a bank? Banks have a long, proud history of being able to size up a potential borrower for their likely ability to handle and repay a loan. They're not stupid. They have hideously complex formulas and processes…that tend to work. It's how they are so profitable.

Absolutely, you can get yourself into fit-and-fighting mortgage shape by yourself. And, in fact, much of it you have to do yourself, such as the budgeting and saving a deposit. And you can do the whole loan research and application process yourself too.

But some people who want to do it themselves often find it gets too hard or find that their situation requires some negotiation or lender policy knowledge to get the loan through. By all means, if doing thorough research is your thing, go ahead. But if you get to a point where you're feeling out of your depth…stop and get someone in.

You can do some real damage to your credit record by applying for loans and having them knocked back. Every application for credit goes on your credit file. And the more knockbacks you have, the harder it gets to explain to the next lender.

If your life is too short, get professional help. Good brokers can usually also help with other professionals you might need too, such as conveyancing solicitors and insurers.

And just to ram it home ... here are the key points to take away from this chapter.

- Getting mortgage fit involves budgeting and saving for a deposit.
- A bank's approval depends on many things, including credit reports, income, work and savings history and other credit limits.
- Debt can be dumb, okay or great, and it's important to know which is which.
- Tax-deductible debt can be great; dumb debt should be paid down immediately.
- Getting loan approvals requires thorough paperwork.
- Lending rules vary from bank to bank.
- Pre-approval of loans can be very helpful, but it is not foolproof.
- Guarantors can be of assistance in some circumstances, but it's usually best to be in a position where you don't need them.
- Stamp duty varies wildly from state to state, as do bonuses and handouts for first-home buyers.
- Whether to DIY or go with a mortgage broker is an important decision.
- It is important for your mortgage broker to be transparent about commissions and conflicts of interest.

4

The loan ranger—understanding mortgages

I think my own love of property began with the world's greatest game of greed—Monopoly. If you want your kids to understand the power that property can bring, get them hooked on Monopoly. My kids are at that age now. And they WILL learn to love it!

Monopoly teaches you the nuts and bolts of property. It's not the real deal. Building a property portfolio in real life is whole lot more complex than landing on a property, checking your pile of cash and saying 'yep, I'll buy Vine Street, thanks'. In the game, you must buy real estate with cash—you can't borrow from the bank. You can mortgage post-purchase, but there's a flat interest rate of 10 per cent.

There's no stamp duty. The tax office doesn't help out with deductions. You're never faced with tenant dramas, like the hot water service blowing up, or the air conditioner needing replacement. Tenants only pay rent once, then nick off. And, dammit, there's no negative gearing!

There's little of the complexity that comes with loans in real life, where the number of products is flabbergasting and seems to expand to more new frontiers than a *Star Trek* expedition.

So, let's rip into the crucial detail on the big choices you face when taking out a loan. Here's what you need to know about lenders, their standard terms and products, the optional extras and *buying banking in bulk*—the benefits of scale from having multiple properties.

Which bank?

For a start, they're not all banks. And while the Commonwealth Bank ('Which Bank?') is still the biggest home lender in the country, it's in an increasingly crowded space, where it's having to compete like everyone else.

The majority of loans will come from four main categories of lenders—banks, building societies, credit unions and non-bank lenders.

In decades past, there were important distinctions between the different types of lenders. Many of those differentiators are long-since gone. No longer are they completely dependent on their customers' savings to lend out to property purchasers. While that is still a significant source of capital for them, they are all increasingly reliant on sourcing funds via *securitisation*—that is, from investors.

Australia's Big Four banks are ANZ Bank, Commonwealth Bank of Australia (CBA), National Australia Bank and Westpac. They are known as the *Four Pillars* because they are protected, to a degree, by a government policy banning them from merging.

Most of them also own other bank brands. For instance, CBA owns BankWest, NAB has NAB Broker (formerly HomeSide), and Westpac has St George, Bank of Melbourne and Bank of South Australia.

In the second tier are smaller national and regional banks, including Macquarie Bank, Bank of Queensland, AMP, Adelaide Bank, Bendigo Bank, Suncorp Metway and Members Equity Bank. There are many foreign-owned banks also, including Citibank, HSBC, Royal Bank of Scotland, and banks without branches, including ING Direct and Rabobank.

There aren't many building societies and credit unions left in Australia, due to mergers, though there are a few big names left, including Greater Building Society, IMB, Newcastle Permanent, The Rock Building Society, Australian Defence Credit Union and Credit Union Australia.

And then there are the non-bank lenders, including the likes of Aussie Home Loans (owned by CBA), Pepper and Virgin Home Loans.

The internet has given even small lenders the ability to play nationally. You can go direct through a lender, and brokers often have access to small lenders.

When it comes to choosing a lender to work with regarding your property ambitions, my preference is for institutions whose name you know and trust — those with reputations to protect.

If you're unsure about the options, see a mortgage broker, who will have a better idea of which lenders are reputable to deal with. Most people who seek a loan will have a choice of many lenders to work with and it will be a case of using the one that provides the services that you want to use, at the best possible interest rate. Others, who might not have the same choice because of their personal circumstances, might only have a couple of lenders who will work with them.

In many cases, the choices you face are a case of six of one versus half a dozen of another. In other cases, it might be whether or not you wish to use a particular function or not.

Let's get started!

Loans — making the big decisions in the right order

Despite the fuss that is made about them in the media, interest rates are not the only factor in choosing a home loan. They're an important part, sure. But they're just the price that you pay for a service. Competition, at a given moment, will determine what that price is. Interest rates change. Lenders play games with rates. Good discounts now can look shabby (or even better) a few years down the track. Your rate is something to review regularly.

Most property buyers will find that many major lenders will compete and even fall over themselves to get their business, and will end up within a poofteenth of each other on rates.

Getting the interest rate wrong by a little bit will do far less damage to your finances than getting some other important structural issues wrong. Don't believe me? Read through the rest of this chapter and I'll show you.

Picking a lender on interest rates alone is putting the cart before the horse, or Hutch before Starsky.

You need to determine the most suitable loan structure first. Loan structure errors will be far more costly than the few bucks a month you'll save on a cheaper loan.

Here are the questions you need to answer first.

- What are you trying to achieve with your property purchase? (It's very different for a homebuyer versus investor.)

- Should you be paying principal and interest, or interest-only?

- Might this home one day become an investment property?

- Does your career mean that you should have an eye to asset protection?

Repay the loan — or hold on to your capital?

The first big choice when it comes to a property loan is whether you wish to pay principal and interest (P&I) or interest-only (I/O).

Principal and interest (P&I) loans

Principal and interest loans are the standard. A P&I loan involves paying back the original amount borrowed. Over the course of a 25- or 30-year loan, you will slowly pay back the amount originally borrowed.

In the first few years of a P&I mortgage, most of the repayment is actually to cover interest. As the loan continues, and the principal is slowly paid down, more and more of the monthly (or weekly or fortnightly) repayments go to reducing the capital.

This is a process called amortisation, where the interest is calculated on the outstanding loan balance. As the loan balance reduces, the amount that is ascribed to principal increases, as opposed to interest, which decreases. This is set out in table 4.1 and figure 4.1 (on p. 54). While repayments stay constant throughout the loan term, in the first year of the loan, only $4471 of all payments goes to paying down the loan itself. In year 15, $11 079 goes towards paying off the principal and in the final year, $29 028 goes to paying off the principal. Over the same time frames, the interest payments fall from $25 868 in year one, to $19 260 in year 15 and just $1042 in year 30.

Table 4.1: amortisation of $400 000 loan

Year	Cumulative Payments Principal	Cumulative Payments Interest	Loan Balance	Principal reduction	Interest payments
0	$0	$0	$400 000		
1	$4 471	$25 868	$395 529	$4 471	$25 868
2	$9 241	$51 437	$390 759	$4 770	$25 569
3	$14 331	$76 687	$385 669	$5 090	$25 250
4	$19 762	$101 595	$380 238	$5 431	$24 908
5	$25 556	$126 140	$374 444	$5 794	$24 545
6	$31 739	$150 297	$368 261	$6 183	$24 157
7	$38 335	$174 040	$361 665	$6 596	$23 743
8	$45 373	$197 341	$354 627	$7 038	$23 301
9	$52 883	$220 170	$347 117	$7 510	$22 829
10	$60 895	$242 497	$339 105	$8 012	$22 327
11	$69 445	$264 287	$330 555	$8 550	$21 790
12	$78 566	$285 505	$321 434	$9 121	$21 218
13	$88 299	$306 111	$311 701	$9 733	$20 606
14	$98 684	$326 066	$301 316	$10 385	$19 955
15	$109 763	$345 326	$290 237	$11 079	$19 260
16	$121 585	$363 843	$278 415	$11 822	$18 517
17	$134 199	$381 568	$265 801	$12 614	$17 725
18	$147 658	$398 449	$252 342	$13 459	$16 881
19	$162 017	$414 429	$237 983	$14 359	$15 980
20	$177 339	$429 446	$222 661	$15 322	$15 017
21	$193 686	$443 438	$206 314	$16 347	$13 992
22	$211 129	$456 335	$188 871	$17 443	$12 897
23	$229 740	$468 064	$170 260	$18 611	$11 729
24	$249 597	$478 546	$150 403	$19 857	$10 482
25	$270 783	$487 698	$129 217	$21 186	$9 152
26	$293 389	$495 432	$106 611	$22 606	$7 734
27	$317 509	$501 651	$82 491	$24 120	$6 219
28	$343 244	$506 256	$56 756	$25 735	$4 605
29	$370 702	$509 136	$29 298	$27 458	$2 880
30	$400 000	$510 178	$0	$29 298	$1 042

Figure 4.1: principal and interest loan amortisation

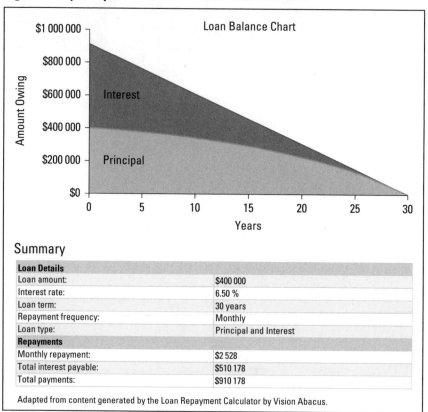

Summary

Loan Details	
Loan amount:	$400 000
Interest rate:	6.50 %
Loan term:	30 years
Repayment frequency:	Monthly
Loan type:	Principal and Interest
Repayments	
Monthly repayment:	$2 528
Total interest payable:	$510 178
Total payments:	$910 178

Adapted from content generated by the Loan Repayment Calculator by Vision Abacus.

Property equity is built in two ways. The first, and easiest (and let's deal with big, round numbers here, to keep things reasonably simple), is usually as the property increases in value (say from $500 000 to $700 000). The second is for the loan to be paid down (say from $400 000 to $350 000). In this example, the property owner's equity has increased from $100 000 at purchase ($500 000 less $400 000) to $350 000 ($700 000 less $350 000).

If this property is going to be your home for a long time (or you would sell it when moving to your next home), then a P&I loan is likely to be your best bet.

Interest-only (I/O) loans

With interest-only, you pay only the interest. If you borrowed $400 000 on an interest-only loan for five years, then after five years you would still owe the bank $400 000.

It's that simple. If you take out a loan for $450 000 at 6 per cent, then you will pay interest of $27 000 a year, or an average of $2250 a month (it will vary according to the number of days in the month).

Some people look at interest-only loans and say: 'Why would you do that? Don't you want to repay the loan?'

Simply, in some situations, the answer is 'no'. Interest-only loans keep your repayments lower and can be more efficient (for cashflow and tax) for those who have both a tax-deductible investment property loan and a non-deductible home loan.

In that example, it might be better to pay just the interest on your investment loan, allowing you to redirect your spare capital to faster repayment of your own home loan.

In fact, for property investors, it rarely makes sense for them to be doing anything but interest-only loans when they still have a home loan. By paying interest-only, you keep your investment debt (a tax deduction) as high as possible, while reducing your non-deductible debt (your home loan) faster, with the aid of offset and redraw accounts (see later in this chapter).

Fixed rate or variable?

The next big choice is Shakespearean: 'To fix, or not to fix?' Are you prepared to have your monthly mortgage repayment fluctuate with a variable loan, or would you prefer to know, from month to month, your exact repayments?

In Australia, variable rate loans are the norm. About 80 to 90 per cent of all loans in Australia are variable, with the remainder of loans being fixed. (Interestingly, in the United States the situation is the exact opposite. Between 80 and 90 per cent of their loans are fixed.)

Variable rate loans

A variable rate loan means you are at the mercy of the interest rate gods (the senior ranking deity is the Reserve Bank). If interest rates go up, your repayments will rise. If rates fall, your repayments will drop.

For example, a variable rate loan might be 6.25 per cent. If the Reserve Bank of Australia (RBA) were to lift rates by 0.25 percentage points, then your bank is likely to lift your interest rate to 6.5 per cent. In that example, for a $400 000, 30-year loan, your repayments would rise from $2462.87 to $2528.27, an increase of $65.40 a month.

In general, surveys have shown that in Australia, variable rate loans tend to be cheaper, over the course of a full interest rate cycle, by around 0.3 per cent. I list the main advantages and disadvantages of variable and fixed loans in table 4.2.

Table 4.2: variable versus fixed rates

Variable rate — advantages	Fixed rate — advantages
Flexibility to make extra repayments	Monthly repayments are known
Ability to redraw	No regular adjustments to your repayments
Ability to use offset account to make the most of extra savings	Easier to plan for
Tends to be lower over the long run	
Variable rate — disadvantages	**Fixed rate — disadvantages**
Mortgage repayments can change at any time	Limited ability to make extra repayments
No protection from rising interest rates	If interest rates fall, you will be stuck with higher repayments
	Lack of flexibility — exit fees can be stiff
	Usually no benefit from an offset account

Fixed rate loans

A fixed rate loan is a bit like a security blanket (I'm thinking Linus from *Peanuts*). You are fixing your rate for a set period of time (usually one to ten years, with two, three and five years being standard). As a result, you know exactly what your repayments are going to be.

If you fix a loan at 6.5 per cent ($420 000, P&I) for three years, your repayments are going to be $2654.69 a month, each month, for the next three years.

As a concept, fixed repayments are appealing — particularly for first-home buyers. And, sure, fixed rates have their benefits. However, they have their downsides also. They can be very rigid. You might not be able to make extra repayments and you probably won't be able to make use of an offset account. And if you decide that your situation has changed, or you want to sell, you might face very high exit fees if rates have fallen since you fixed your loan.

Slicing and dicing — a bet each way

But you can, with most lenders, be half-pregnant on this one. You can opt to go part-variable, and benefit from the likes of offset and redraw accounts and extra repayments, and part-fixed.

You could go 50-50, or fix a higher or lower percentage of your loan, to suit your situation.

This is often a great solution for those who want some surety. Lock up some in a fixed rate loan, leaving a portion variable so that you can pay ahead on your mortgage.

If you had to break the fixed rate loan for any reason, you would still likely face exit fees.

Offset accounts — the greatest savings account in our solar system

Offset accounts have been around for decades now. But their power is still not well understood. An offset account is a very powerful tool in the battle to own your home sooner. Having an offset account attached to your home loan is virtually a must for anyone capable of saving above and beyond their monthly mortgage repayments.

An offset account is a savings account, but one with a difference. Whatever amount of money you have in your offset account — be that $1000, $10 000 or $100 000 — will save you interest on your mortgage. And this is, literally, twice as powerful a tool as earning interest (see the text box overleaf).

How does it work? If you have a home loan of $380000 and you have savings of $30000 in your offset account, then you will pay interest for the month on just $350000 ($380000 minus $30000). On a 6.25 per cent home loan, your $30000 has just saved you $156.25 for the month. Have that $30000 sitting there for the entire year and it will save you $1875. As a bonus, you pay no tax on these savings.

Offsets — *TWICE* as powerful as a savings account

Let's say you have a mortgage of $470000. Your mortgage interest rate is 6 per cent. You also have $50000 in savings. The interest, in a high-interest online account, is 4 per cent.

If you have your $50000 sitting in that high-interest account, you will earn $2000 interest over a year. If you earn a salary of $100000 a year, you will then have to pay approximately $780 (assuming a marginal tax rate of 39 per cent), leaving you with net earnings on your $2000 of $1220. That's a net return of just 2.46 per cent.

Now, let's put that $50000 in an offset account. You're *saving* interest at 6 per cent. Over a year, that $50000 would save you $3000 in interest.

But because offset savings are interest *saved* and not earned, *there is no tax to pay*. So you get to keep the whole $3000. Often, you don't usually see it, but it has reduced your mortgage by $3000, which will compound in savings over the remainder of your home loan.

In this case, the $3000 is almost 150 per cent better than the $1230 gained from earning interest at 4 per cent.

For those on higher incomes (above $180000) the savings are even bigger. But anyone who pays income tax and has savings (and a mortgage of course) will generally benefit from proper use of an offset account.

So, given their power, how do you make the most of offset accounts? (I'll talk about their cousins, redraw accounts, shortly.)

Simple. Every single spare cent you have should sit in your offset account. Get all of your income directed to your offset account—salaries, share dividends, rent from investment properties, birthday money, lucky punts at the track...everything.

Multiple offset accounts—'yours, mine and ours'

In the 1990s came the first offset accounts. The first ones weren't great and often only gave a partial offset on your mortgage.

Then came the full offset account, where every cent fully offset interest payments on the loan account. However, each banking product, or loan, usually only had one offset account.

In recent years, some lenders have started offering *multiple offset accounts*, with the balances on multiple accounts all adding up to offset against a main home loan.

This is a fantastic innovation, particularly for couples who have separate finances. They could have, for example, three offset accounts. One for him, one for her and then one for their joint finances. If he had $3000 in his account, she had $7000 in her account and their 'ours' account had a further $8000 in it, then they would have a total of $18 000 offsetting against their interest bill for the month.

And leave your funds in the offset accounts for as long as possible. Pay your bills at the last minute. Better still, use the credit card plus offset account combination (see later this chapter) to squeeze an extra few hundred dollars a year in extra savings.

If you can operate with a bit of a buffer—without being tempted to spend it—you would work your offset account in the following way. If you have a home loan, you would have all income coming into it. Figure 4.2 (overleaf) shows how savings of $30 000 reduce the amount of interest paid on a $150 000 loan, while table 4.3 (overleaf) shows you the sort of income that you should have paid into your actual account—that is, everything. If there is an average of $30 000 in the account for the month, then the property owner would only pay interest on $120 000 for the month.

Figure 4.2: how offset accounts save you money

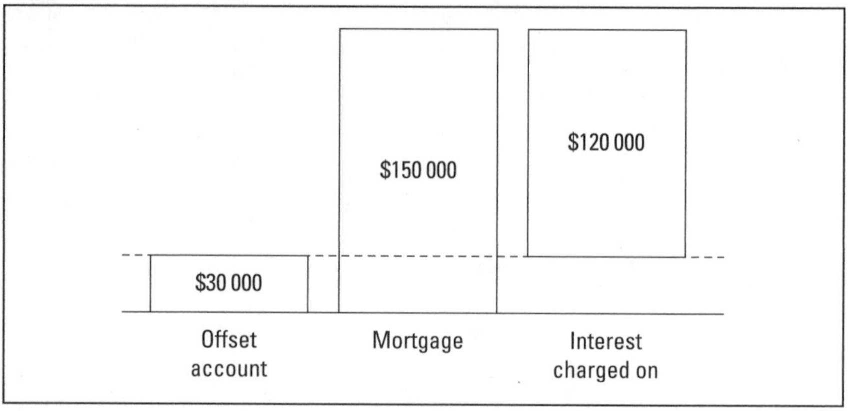

Table 4.3: maximising your offset account—ins and outs

Incoming	Outgoing
Salaries	Mortgage
Dividends	Credit card repayment (direct debited, on last day)
Tax refunds	Direct debit bills (on last day)
Rent received (from investment properties)	Low cash holdings in your wallet

Turning a home into an investment property?

If you are buying a home, and there's a chance you might turn it into an investment property as you upgrade within a couple of years, then consider a combination of an interest-only loan with an offset account.

There are two very important reasons for this. The first is about keeping the loan balance high for future tax deductions. The second is about the ATO's views about the difference between offset and redraw accounts.

With an interest-only loan, use the offset account to build up your savings. This will reduce your monthly interest charge on the loan. But it would also leave you in a position where you could take your equity (savings in your offset account) with you to your next property. There are important tax reasons for this, explained in chapter 7.

For example: You have purchased a house worth $500000, with a loan of $450000. Over the course of two years, you have managed to lift the balance in your offset account from $10000 in the first month to $100000 at the end of two years.

In month one, you were paying interest on $440000 ($450000 less $10000), while at the end of two years, you were paying interest on $350000 ($450000 less $100000).

You decide to buy a bigger home, but wish to turn your current home into an investment property. Because your savings are in an offset account, you can take the $100000 to the new house, and you will receive a tax deduction on the full $450000 of the loan again, as the loan itself was never less than $450000.

Second, from the ATO's perspective, there is a massive difference between a redraw and an offset account.

An offset account is a savings account. It's your money. No question. What you do with it is your business.

A redraw account is different. Money in a redraw account is money you have *repaid* on your loan. The ATO's view is that if you are taking money from a redraw account, you are taking money back out of the loan from the bank. And they will only allow you to claim a deduction on the lowest amount your loan reached.

Here is how this becomes important.

Let's say Sarah and Ruth both have homes worth $500000. They both originally took out loans for $400000. On top of that, they each have $100000 in savings.

Sarah has a loan for $400000, *offset* by $100000 savings, so she would pay interest on $300000. The ATO sees it as a $400000 loan, because the offset account is separate money.

Ruth, however, has $100000 in her *redraw* account. The ATO sees this as a loan for $300000, with $0 savings.

Ruth and Sarah then turn their homes into investment properties and rent them out, purchasing new homes using their $100000 cash as deposits.

The will end up with very different tax positions.

Sarah will be able to claim a tax deduction on the entire $400000 loan. Ruth, however, will still have a loan of $400000, but the ATO will only allow her to claim a deduction on $300000, as that was the lowest point her loan got to before she turned it into an investment property.

Redraw accounts—paying it back early

From an interest-saving perspective, a redraw account does exactly the same job as a true offset account. But the treatment of the money is slightly different.

A redraw account is where your extra loan repayments go. Not all banks or bank products offer redraw accounts. But if they do, then the money you have over your monthly mortgage sits in redraw.

For example, if your monthly loan repayment is $2200, but you instead pay $3200 ($1000 extra), at the end of 12 months, you will have $12 000 sitting in your redraw account. Most banks will allow you to redraw that $12 000 as you wish (some might charge a fee, or insist on a minimum being redrawn).

At the end of that 12 months, you will also be saving yourself interest on $12 000 each month. At 6.5 per cent, that's a saving of $65 a month, each and every month.

A redraw account is useful in a number of ways:

- it gives you a better sense of achievement in paying down your loan

- it is a good place to 'hide' savings, as it normally won't appear as a balance when you pull money from an ATM

- you are probably less likely to spend what's in it than when your funds are in your savings/offset account

- if you are in your home and you are sure you won't ever want to convert your home into an investment property, then a redraw account will usually be a better option for long-term savings than an offset account.

However, if there is a good chance, or even a rough chance, that you will want to turn your home into an investment property in the future, then you may want to consider the advice in the text box entitled *Turning a home into an investment property?* (p. 60) in regards to using an offset account instead of a redraw account.

Redraw accounts are not parking lots

One couple I know had an investment property in Melbourne. They lived interstate and were 'between' homes, as they were building their dream home, which was a nine-month build. For that period, they had no mortgage and were renting.

During that time, they received an inheritance, which they intended to use to keep the mortgage on the new dream house to a minimum when completed. Unfortunately, they parked the $150 000 in the rental property's redraw account, reducing the loan from $180 000 to $30 000.

Their accountant informed them they could now only claim a tax deduction on $30 000, even if they redrew the money for their new home, because of the ATO's opinion of redraw accounts. For investors, parking the money in a redraw account can have dreadful tax consequences.

It was a disaster for their tax position for that property. Unfortunately, it then made clear sense for them to sell the property and purchase a new investment property. A costly exercise, as sales and agents fees needed to be paid, plus stamp duty on the new property.

Terms—25 or 30 years?

How long should your home loan be for? Aim for a 25-year home loan, in the hope of paying it off faster? Or a 30-year term, making repayments slightly more affordable?

With the availability of offset and redraw accounts, this question is now almost irrelevant. Most banks now offer 30-year terms by default. There is so much flexibility in most banking products now that the loan term is somewhat immaterial. Almost no-one holds a loan for 30 years anymore.

It does make a difference to repayments. A $400 000 loan with a 25-year loan term has monthly P&I repayments of $2700.83, while for a 30-year term, it would be $2528.27—a difference of $172.56 a month. For some, this could could be the difference between being able to afford a loan or not.

Largely because of redraw and offset accounts, taking a 30-year loan term will keep your options open wider. You can still pay it off in 25, or 15, years, if you wish.

And now ... interest rates

Interest rates! Right! You'd nearly forgotten about them, hadn't you?

In the order of importance, this is roughly where interest rates sit. Absolutely. Dead. Serious. The questions prior to here were about finding the right structure for your lending product. Getting that right will save you far more than interest rates, which are almost always negotiable with a lender.

There's no point having a great rate if it's going to cost you more than you're saving because it's a no-frills banking product. And if you find a product that suits you perfectly, but the rate is a little higher, then haggle with them (or get a broker to do it for you).

An interest rate is the cost of borrowing, or renting, money when you don't have enough cash to buy something yourself. It's the biggest cost of buying a property and will cost you hundreds of thousands of dollars over the course of a 25- or 30-year loan.

The setting of interest rates is quite complex. But here it is in a nutshell.

It starts with the Reserve Bank of Australia. The RBA sets the overnight lending rate between banks. This interest rate is the single largest influence on other lending rates, particularly for property (and business) loans. That is, if the RBA is moving the *official cash rate* up, your mortgage rate is also likely to increase. If the RBA is cutting rates, then your lender will likely reduce your interest rate. Before the GFC, banks would move their rates in lock step with the RBA. Post-GFC, they move a little more independently.

The banks have a headline rate, broadly known as the *standard variable rate* (SVR). Almost nobody pays the SVR on their home loan. As a mortgage rate, it's mythical. Particularly when it comes to lending for residential properties, borrowers receive a discount from the SVR.

At the time of writing, those discounts vary from around 0.5 per cent through to as much as 1.4 per cent (for those with very large loan balances with their lender).

RBA versus SVR versus discounted rates—what does it mean?

At the time of writing, the Reserve Bank's official cash rate was at 2.5 per cent (a 50-plus-year low). The average SVR of the Big Four banks was approximately 5.9 per cent. The average discount, for someone with total loans of approximately $500000, would be around 0.9 per cent to 1 per cent. So, the interest rate that they're paying? They would be paying an interest rate of approximately 4.9 per cent to 5 per cent, give or take some negotiation.

Those who had bigger loans and were in a position to negotiate as customers with strong financials could have been up for an interest rate of as low as about 4.7 per cent, being a discount of approximately 1.2 per cent off the bank's average SVR.

On average, the RBA will move rates a few times a year, depending on the health of the economy. If the economy is running strong, the RBA will generally increase interest rates. If the economy is cooling, the RBA will usually cut rates to try to stimulate demand by putting more money into people's pockets.

At any one time, the Big Four banks have about 80 per cent of the market. They continually jostle with each other for market share. But they also have to deal with the rising competition from smaller players.

What's the cost of not getting your interest rate right? If you're taking out a $400000 loan for a home or an investment property for 30 years at 6.5 per cent, you will pay nearly $26000 in interest alone in the first year. If you manage to negotiate a rate of 6.3 per cent, you would pay around $25200—a saving of around $800.

The interest rate charged by your lender is, obviously, important. The lower it is, the better. For some borrowers, a low rate is the only thing that matters. Saving a few extra dollars a week is money in their pocket and not the bank's.

Fighting for a good rate is important. But there will come a point where leaving one lender to save an extra 0.05 per cent a year could actually cost you money. Perhaps they don't offer offset accounts, or you are going to be charged to use other banks' ATM networks. Banks reward loyal, large customers. And if you've got $1 million in loans with a bank, you're a large customer. How loyal you stay should depend on how well they treat you.

If you find two lenders that are within, say, 0.05 per cent of each other, but the one with the lower interest rate doesn't have something you would find value in, then you will often be better off paying the higher rate. Not always. But these are the finer points that really make a brilliant home loan deal.

Construction loans

Building a home or doing a big renovation is an exciting prospect for many Australians. But designing your dream home and constructing it with a builder can also be daunting.

And, of course, financing a build or big renovation is not straightforward. In most states, there are strict rules about when payments for building works, known as *progress payments*, should be made. Progress payments will cover various stages of the building process, including land, pad (potentially the slab, plus joists and bearers, for example), roof, lock-up and final. As each stage is reached, a new progress payment is made to the builder.

While you might have got approval for a loan of $380 000 or so, progress payments mean that you will only have to pay interest as the payments are made to the builder.

Not all lenders offer construction loans. Make sure you do your research on this aspect first, or speak to a quality mortgage broker.

Lines of credit—a blessing and a curse

A line of credit is a flexible lending product where the bank approves a facility for you to use at your discretion.

They can be particularly useful when used for investment purposes, as they give you the flexibility to make payments when required and as quickly as you can organise a bank transfer. They are often used as an add-on to another lending product.

For example, let's say a family has an $800 000 home, with a $200 000 mortgage. They want flexibility for further property or share investment.

They could take a line of credit against their home for, say, $200 000, that sits unused until required. There's no interest paid until they draw down on the loan. But when they see a suitable property, they can quickly access the funds from the line of credit to pay the deposit.

They can be a very useful tool for investors.

However, danger lurks with lines of credit in that they don't come with rules from the lender. That is, you have unfettered access up to the limit of your line of credit to spend. Many give in to the dark side and are sadly tempted to use that money for consumer goods, thereby spending money, and racking up debt, on things they couldn't have otherwise afforded, which fits into the *dumb debt* category.

Equity ma-a-a-te!

The Commonwealth Bank came up with a catchy advertising campaign with its 'Equity Mate' commercials in the 1990s. The ads showed a guy in a new boat in his driveway, with a neighbour asking him how he afforded the boat. His answer, with one of the biggest grins ever seen on Australian television, was 'Equity ma-a-a-ate!'

The campaign proved a mixed result for CBA. It was a catchy ad that launched the bank into the space and made Australians aware that the equity in their home could be used. But it also copped criticism for encouraging Australians to access home equity to fund consumables. From a financial planning perspective, it sent out a bad message—that it's okay to blow the equity you've built in your home to buy depreciating assets, or to fund holidays and other lifestyle choices.

Professional packages

Professional packages, or pro-packs, are offered by most major lenders and usually come with an annual fee, usually of between $200 and $400 a year.

When they first started, pro-packs were literally for professionals, or those earning above a certain income. Those rules have long since gone and most pro-packs now are actually tied to loan amounts.

For your annual pro-pack fee, you might be offered some of the following features:

- a minimum discount on the bank's standard variable rate
- discounts on fixed loan rates
- $0 loan establishment fees
- account fee waivers
- no top-up, portability or switching fees
- free credit cards
- free loyalty program memberships
- free cheque accounts
- free travel insurance
- discounts on financial advice through the bank's financial planning arm, including superannuation and life insurances
- discounts on general insurance products, including home-and-contents and landlord's insurance
- free share brokerage.

Individual pro-pack offers differ widely, but these are the sorts of benefits offered. Often, the major lenders will entice people to sign up for pro-packs based solely on the discounted home loans on offer, but it may be worth considering them for their other benefits also.

Credit cards

Credit cards have grown in importance and sophistication since Bankcard was introduced to Australia in the 1970s. Some people can't live without one. Others find them moderately useful. And a whole bunch of Australians would be better off without them. For the latter, credit cards can cause real financial hardship.

Credit cards come with limits that you can spend up to. As discussed in chapter 3, credit cards can be your friend — if you use them properly and pay the balance off in full each month.

Most major lenders will offer a free credit card as part of their loans package, often through a professional package. And depending on your spending habits and what sort of card suits you best, having a free credit card to assist with managing your money can be valuable.

For those wanting to make the most of their banking relationship, it can make sense to have a credit card paid in full by direct debit, on the last day, from your offset account—thereby using the maximum number of interest-free days on your card and leaving money in your offset account, saving you on interest.

But others, those who find that they constantly owe money on their credit cards, might be better off with an ultra-low-rate home loan without a free credit card.

Tip—don't go overboard on credit cards

Credit cards can cause carnage for those who can't control their spending. They can be too easy to get and, once received, many find it is simply too easy to spend. It can be difficult, but if you're constantly finding that you aren't paying off your credit card in full every month, the solution is not to get access to further credit by getting another credit card.

If you find that you occasionally need to go up to, say, $5000 on your card, keep cards with limits of, perhaps, $8000. If you don't need $25 000 worth of credit card limits, call the bank and get your limit cut.

See chapter 3 for more on how much even an extra $10 000 in credit card limits can affect your ability to borrow money from a lender.

The 1 percenters—combining offset accounts and credit cards

Paying your bills via credit card can give an offset account even more bang for its already incredibly powerful buck.

How? Let's say the statement for your credit card is due on the twentieth of each month and you have an automatic full 'sweep' payment of your credit card done each month, so that it's automatically paid from your offset account on the final day that payment is due.

(continued)

The 1 percenters — combining offset accounts and credit cards *(cont'd)*

You've got a few bills due (electricity, gas, rates, and so on), worth a total of $1000, on the twenty-third, twenty-fourth and twenty-sixth. If you delay paying those bills until after the twentieth and then put them on your credit card, you will then get to keep $1000 in your account for an extra month, as they will go on the next bill.

Having that extra $1000 in your offset account for an extra month at a 6 per cent interest rate will save you $5 for the month. Done for the whole year, it would be $60.

If you use your credit card for almost everything, but ensure it's paid off in full EVERY SINGLE MONTH, this strategy can save you hundreds of dollars each year. If this is all set up for automatic payments, then it's saving you time and money while you're sleeping.

This makes less sense, possibly no sense, if there is a charge for using a credit card to pay those bills. Even a charge of 0.5 per cent or so can defeat the purpose. Why? A 0.5 per cent charge on your money for, say, seven days, is the equivalent of being charged 26 per cent for the whole year. Not worth it. Use a free option.

ATM access

We haven't hit the cashless society yet—you still need access to the folding stuff. You need to be able to pull money out of a branch, a hole-in-the-wall (ATM) or from a supermarket. Cash, currently, is still often more convenient for buying a sandwich or a coffee.

Nowadays, there are ATMs every 50 metres on a busy street—except, of course, when you need one.

But not all lenders have their own ATM networks. The Big Four banks have them everywhere, but the second- and third-tier lenders often don't have any at all. Would you drive across town to take money out of an ATM to save yourself a $2 ATM fee? No. But if you're constantly getting cash from ATMs, that's going to be costly.

Some people get around this by regularly pulling out extra cash when they go to the supermarket, or fill up with a tank of petrol. But for others, that won't work. And access to an ATM network is a necessity.

Factor into your considerations how you are going to access cash. Some smaller lenders don't have ATM networks, but might have done deals with competitors to offer free or cheap ATM access for their customers. Others won't. You will need to factor these regular fees into your considerations. Alternatively, find a way of changing your habits and how you get cash, such as getting $50 every time you go into a shop.

Buying banking in bulk—million-dollar mortgage portfolios

Okay, if you're hardcore about property—and intending on building a kick-butt property portfolio—listen up.

A property portfolio will come with monstrous debt. For monstrous debt, you're going to want a great relationship with a quality lender, who offers you pricing and service that match your value to them as a borrower.

If you have a home and one investment property, debt of more than $1 million would not be unheard of.

If you have three or four investment properties, plus a home, your debt could easily top $2 million. Once you get into that range, lenders will be very keen for your business. But they might also want more information about you.

If interest rates are 6.5 per cent and you've got $2 million worth of loans, you are paying $130 000 a year in *interest* payments to your bank. Plus, you'll probably have a credit card or two and might also have car loans, margin loans and substantial savings too.

That's a big client for a bank and they should sharpen their pencil for you. Demand the best rates. They'll do what they need to do to keep you, if you're generally a good customer.

But big property portfolios might also require you to diversify your banking partners. See chapter 7 for more on structuring loans on bigger portfolios.

Managing multiple mortgages

Property investment can quickly produce a menagerie of mortgages. You could have three properties, but five to six loans, depending on how you have structured your loans.

For many, the easiest way to track everything would be to have all the loans coming into and out of the one account—and there's nothing wrong with that account being the offset account for your home loan.

The dream offset account set-up

If you've got a home loan and a few investment properties, here's how to maximise tax-effective returns.

Have all income from all sources paid into the offset account for your home loan. If you've got two lots of rent (say, $1800 and $2200) coming in on the first of the month, but repayments for the associated loans aren't due until, say, the eighteenth, then you'll have that $4000 working to save you every month for an extra 18 days.

Get your salaries directly credited to that account also. If you have any shares paying dividends, get them paid here too.

Pay for everything you possibly can (but only spending what you normally would) on a credit card where the full balance is automatically paid on the last due date, thereby permanently keeping thousands of extra dollars in the offset account until the last due date.

Have any loans paid from this account. The bank will take it on the due date, again leaving your money sitting there for the maximum possible time.

Using these strategies could see you permanently have an extra $5000, $10000 or $20000 sitting in your offset, saving you interest on your home loan. An extra $5000 working for you in this way would save you ten months on a 30-year, $300000 home loan at 6.25 per cent.

In order to do this, you need to have a consistent float. The more properties you have, the more loans you have, the bigger the float you'll need.

And with so much money flying into and out of one account, it can get confusing. (But at least you're just managing one account). And this might be too much for some people who prefer to have money compartmentalised. Some will like to have all of their loans and rental payments separate, to avoid temptation. If the extra effort of organising that is going to be worth it, and will make it easier for you to keep track of where you're at financially, then stick with it. However, in table 4.4 I show you how you can potentially make the most financially of these two products, which can potentially save home buyers and investors thousands of dollars a year.

Table 4.4: dream account set-up for property owner/investor

Offset (savings) account	Redraw account	Credit card
All income paid here, including salary, rent, dividends, etc.	Long-term savings (or to other offset accounts, if you have more than one)	All bills without surcharges paid on card
Direct debits (for bills that have credit card surcharges) paid from here		Paid in full on last day of no interest

Test your lender — threats, ultimatums and tantrums

If you've owned your home for a while and you've been reading this chapter thinking 'Hang on, I should be getting a better deal from my bank' … you're probably right.

No bank has ever written to a client and said 'We'd like to reduce your mortgage rate because we like you'. (Sure, I couldn't possibly know if that statement is true. It's a grand overstatement to make a point. But I'm probably right.) The only time banks ever offer a bigger discount is when you push them.

If you've had a home loan for a while and you haven't demanded your lender show you some loving in recent years, you're probably being taken for a ride.

The bank is looking at your loyalty with part gratefulness, part pity. They are certainly laughing at you. And they do think you're stupid.

You have to put your lender to the test every couple of years. Discounting by banks goes in cycles. It's quite possible that right now, they are offering bigger discounts to new clients than what they offered you when you joined as a customer three to five years ago. Is that fair? No. But a bank is never going to offer you a better rate without a gentle reminder of how good a customer you are. If you're not complaining, you must be happy. If you want a better deal, you need to have a whinge, chuck a tantrum, or make them a threat they can't ignore.

How much is on offer? Depends on how much you owe them. But for example, it could be $2000 a year on a $500 000 loan.

Here's what you do. Find out your home-loan interest rate. Work out your discount. If you can see your bank offering bigger discounts than what you're on currently, they've got a case to answer.

If you want to short-circuit the process, call your bank and ask for a payout figure. Tell them you have been offered a better rate by another bank. If the person on the phone has had any training, they will alert the 'retention' team. You should be called back within a day or so. And if they don't offer you a discount to stay, you'll know they don't value your business anyway.

If you don't know what you're doing or you don't have the confidence to put on the boxing gloves with your bank, 'do yourself a favour' (as Molly Meldrum would say) and get a mortgage broker fighting for you.

Brokers know which banks are doing what deals. They will know either straight away, or can find out quickly, which bank will likely do a deal with you. It's like giving yourself a pay rise. Or a path to owning your home sooner. Or getting a special RBA rate cut, just for you.

Exit fees

Until mid-2011, many lenders had exit fees in place for loans. While this was usually so that they could recover costs from discount entry costs (such as application fees) in the early years, sometimes it was just pure greed.

Anyway, loans taken out after 1 July 2011 can no longer have exit fees. If you have a loan that pre-dates then, and you're planning on moving to another lender, then check with your existing lender first to see whether there are any exit fees to be paid. Get them to put it in writing. It might still make sense to move your loan, but you want to know what that cost is first.

Loan-to-valuation ratios (LVR)

In more recent years, banks have started offering bigger interest rate discounts to those with lower loan-to-valuation ratios. The ratio of the loan to the property's value is known as the loan-to-valuation ratio, or LVR.

This is largely because of lender's mortgage insurance (or LMI, see chapter 7). On all loans above 80 per cent, lenders charge LMI.

If you have a loan of $535 500 on a property worth $630 000, you have an LVR of 85 per cent. If you have a loan of $275 000 on a property worth $550 000, your LVR is 50 per cent.

Some lenders tier their discounts on rates. If your LVR is below 90, 80 or 70 per cent, you might be in for bigger discounts.

Property purchasing principles

We've covered a lot of ground in this chapter. And you may find it difficult to figure out exactly how it fits in with your situation.

But this is a mortgage broker's bread and butter. And being able to quickly find you suitable loan products that will assist your property ambitions should be second nature to them.

I'm a can-do sort of guy. I like learning new things. But there are certain things in life that I look at and think, 'There's a lot of learning involved in doing that properly and it's something I'll only ever have to do once. So I'll get a professional in to do it.'

In recent times, for example, our side gate needed to be reposted and rehung. I'm sure I could have done it, but it probably would have taken me half a day, plus a trip to the hardware store. Learning to install a new computer software package? Nope, that's a once-off that I don't need to learn. I'll find someone in the office who knows what they're doing.

You can do loans yourself — people do it everyday. And it can be fun if you enjoy research. But it's also one of those jobs that you might only do once, or twice, in a lifetime. And if you're not careful, you're less likely to get it right. Sometimes, those jobs are better off handed to a professional.

And just to ram it home … here are the key points to take away from this chapter.

- The first choice to make in taking out a loan is to determine what sort of lending products will best suit your needs and potentially help you own your property sooner.

- You have to decide whether to go with a principal and interest loan or an interest-only loan; your choice will often depend on whether you're buying a home or an investment property.

- You'll need to decide on a fixed rate loan or a variable loan — or a combination of the two.

- Offset accounts can save you major money and are the most powerful savings accounts available to you.

- Redraw accounts can also be useful, but investors need to be careful when looking at tax implications.

- The term of your mortgage is largely irrelevant these days because of loan product flexibility, with 30 years being the most common.

- Interest rates are important, but are far from the only consideration when looking at loans.

- Construction loans, lines of credit, professional packages and credit cards are other banking tools that may help you improve your finances or pay off your home loan faster.

- ATM access can be a factor in choosing which lenders to work with.

- Large mortgage portfolios can come with extra perks.

- Managing multiple mortgages can be simplified by consolidating repayments to a single account.

- If you've been with your lender for a few years without renegotiating your terms, it's time to test the relationship.

- Exit fees should be taken into consideration on loans that were taken out pre-2011.

- Having a lower loan-to-valuation ratio can get you discounted rates.

5

Home—buying the 'Great Australian Dream'

I love helping people buy property. As a mortgage broker and financial adviser, helping people get into their first property is special.

There's nothing like buying your first home. It's not the same as upgrading to your second home. Saving up the deposit and the sense of achievement that comes with that, getting through the gut-churning negotiation (whether at auction or private sale, or signing contracts with a developer), waiting nervously for approval, packing up your old house and preparing for settlement, and then being able to turn the key and open the front door of your new home ... it's not just special, it's unique. You can only buy your first home once.

It's the sort of experience that money can't buy. Nope, that's wrong. That's exactly what it does.

I remember far more about the raw energy in my stomach when Mrs DebtMan and I successfully bid on our first home than I do about our second home, which cost multiples of the first. I could barely talk on the drive to the house. I parked, got out of the car and was so nervous, I locked my keys in the car.

We had set ourselves two limits. We would be happy to pay anything under $337000. But we were prepared to go that little bit extra, to $343000, if necessary. 'So,' I asked Mrs DebtMan the previous evening, 'if someone bids $344000, we'd be happy to let it go?' She nodded. I agreed. We got it for $336000.

Why did we buy that first home? That particular one?

It suited our then lifestyle.

It was a two-storey Victorian terrace in Richmond. It was an eight-minute train ride to where we spent all our work time (then both at the *Herald Sun*) and most of our play time (restaurants and pubs in and around the city). I could be standing in the kitchen and say 'Oops, better go to work', and be at my desk with change out of 20 minutes. Richmond had a great pub scene and restaurants serving the food of what felt like every country on earth. We were close to friends. The house was 121 years old and needed a bit of work, so we could practice our DIY skills. To my surprise, my home handyman skills were outstandingly ordinary.

Who had money to pay professionals or do renovations? Not us, so weekends were spent on the tools. But I remember heading up to Victoria Street for cheap Vietnamese after long days of painting.

A few years on, DebtBoy and DebtGirl arrived. We met a fantastic group of like-minded parents—who shared our appreciation of a drink or two. We were Richmond people!

It was our perfect inner-city yuppie pad.

Until, roughly, DebtBoy turned three. Growing kids need a backyard to kick a footy. And—allowing for shed, outdoor table, deck and plant beds—ours was less than 10 square metres. The search for bigger digs started. We upgraded to something with a backyard after nine years in that place.

Completely normal stuff. Many of you will have similar stories.

Rent … to the death

Some get sick of renting. Some believe renting is simply paying off someone else's mortgage. Some don't like the lack of security—you can be kicked out with a few months' notice.

But understand this: renting is generally pretty cheap in the short and medium terms. You can generally rent a much nicer house, in a nicer part of town, than you could afford to live in if you had to pay a mortgage.

The important thing about renting is summed up in the following catchy jingle: *If you decide not to buy, you will rent until you die.*

Think about it. Renting is forever. If you don't buy, there is no end to the monthly payments. But buying does have an end. Mortgages do get paid off (usually in way less than the 30 years on the loan contract). And once the mortgage has been killed off, there are only relatively smaller costs, including rates, insurance and the general maintenance of the house.

In a previous book, *Debt Man Walking*, I devoted a chapter to going through the pros and cons of renting versus buying. Renting does have its advantages. And it is *generally* cheaper in major cities, until about the 10- or 15-year mark. After that, rents will usually have risen with inflation to the point where the mortgage would be cheaper than the rent you're paying now.

Rent money—it's not dead money

I don't agree that rent money is dead money. It's cheaper than buying for the first decade or so. You can always rent a nicer place, in a nicer part of town, than you could afford to buy if you had to pay the mortgage. Mortgages do, in the short term, cramp your lifestyle.

But I'm a long-term thinker and believe that most people will be better off if they buy when they can afford to. You can make renting work for you. But it's going to be harder and you're going to have to do a lot more investing to make that decision work.

I'm a complete fan of buying if and when you can afford to.

In my opinion, buying a home is the cornerstone of long-term wealth creation. As you pay down your mortgage and the value of the property grows, you grow equity and security. That equity can then potentially be used to purchase further investment assets, such as further properties and share portfolios. You simply don't have that option of using equity in your home to help fund investments when you're renting.

The only way renting can make long-term financial sense is if you put away the difference between what it is costing you to rent your current digs, versus what the mortgage would be if you'd bought it instead.

That money needs to be invested—in shares and property—and not spent. That's a very difficult discipline to maintain year after year. A mortgage is a far easier discipline, an enforced form of saving, similar to superannuation in many respects.

Articles by 'experts' regularly appear in the media claiming that by investing the difference between renting and a mortgage, you'll be ahead. But I've gone through their numbers. They all seem to ignore the fact that a mortgage is, eventually, paid off, but there is no end to renting.

You've picked up this book, so I'm assuming that you're of the same mindset.

Why, what and where?

What has made you decide to buy your first home? In my case, the decision dawned on me while I was reading a book. A light flickered and I suddenly understood property. It came as a shock, like finding out Darth Vader was Luke's father.

Your world does change when the penny finally drops about home ownership. A life with a mortgage and home ownership is definitely very different to a life of renting.

Exciting, yes. A bit scary, sure. And if you don't have some little panic attacks, check your pulse.

When the penny dropped for me, I had a problem. Mrs DebtMan's finances then were like her handbag now—a Twilight Zone for missing junk. Credit card debt, HECS debt, no savings. Near the home deposit starting line? Nope. Still at the shops purchasing some Nike running gear, on credit, so she could at least look the part? Yup.

If we wanted to get going on our financial future, something needed to change. I challenged her to break her bad money habits in one year—and to my surprise, she smashed it!

What has got you to this point? Is it for financial reasons? Are you sick of the hassles of renting? Do you want some security about where you live? Are you doing it in the belief that owning your own home will, eventually, assist you with your broader financial plans? Or are you just a long-term thinker and you know that a home will eventually be paid off, where rent never is?

It's likely your reasons will be at least one of those. And that's great. They're all great reasons to dive into property ownership.

With *why* answered, we're down to *what* and *where*. Again, only you know the answers.

What sort of place are you going to buy? How many bedrooms/bathrooms do you need? How much living space/yard do you want? Do you want house and land, a townhouse, or an apartment?

And where are you going to buy? Have you picked out a town, suburb, or region?

Your home and where you live should be about filling emotional needs. You should feel safe there. It should be your own version of *The Castle* ('How's the serenity?').

It is likely to be about some, or many, of the following. It's close to:

- work, or employment opportunities
- schools (if you have children)
- family and friends
- the bush/beach lifestyle that you couldn't live without

… or it's a long way from any of those, but you don't mind the commute.

And how much?

At some point, you're going to have to make a decision about how much you're going to spend on your first home. Let me tell you something. The number is likely to be a little bit scary, because it is going to come with a loan that is nearly that big. If the house price itself doesn't scare you, the slightly smaller mortgage probably will.

Don't panic. It's okay. And a decade or so down the track, you'll marvel that you bought the place for that amount. But let's now look at what you need to consider in making the big decision on what you can afford.

Setting your own affordability limit

Underlying any home purchase is affordability. Some places you simply won't be able to afford—no matter how much saving you're capable of. In fact, there are several limits when it comes to what you can personally afford.

'How can there be more than one limit? Surely there's just one?' I hear you ask.

Well, no. There are several. There's black. There's white. And there are at least *Fifty Shades of Grey*—you will need to decide what your limit is. Largely, your limit will be determined by what you are prepared to sacrifice. Some of the limits are obvious and some aren't. But you need to think your way through them to make your own decision.

Some of those limits can be posed as the following questions. Ultimately, how much would the mortgage be if you ...

1   bought the home you would really like?

2   bought a home that would allow you to maintain your current lifestyle?

3   bought a better home and you were prepared to sacrifice some of your current lifestyle?

4   bought an even nicer home and you were prepared to strip back your lifestyle to the basics (at least until you got a few pay rises)?

5   borrowed the maximum a bank would lend you?

Those five questions could produce five different answers. Such as:

1   You saw a recent property sell that was perfect and would leave you with a mortgage of $550000.

2   You've both worked hard and have enjoyed a good lifestyle, while still managing to save a deposit. To maintain that lifestyle, the biggest mortgage you could afford would be $420000.

3   If you sacrificed a little of your lifestyle, you could probably afford a loan of $470000.

4   If you went 'bare bones' lifestyle for a few years, you could potentially go to $560000.

5   A major bank will lend you $750000.

The answer to Question 5 can produce a true shock to many people. Online mortgage calculators often suggest banks will lend a ridiculous amount of money. Is that the amount of money you should borrow? Almost certainly not. But under the right circumstances, some lenders will go that far and some people might be willing to borrow that much, if they want that house.

Which one is the right limit for you? In my experience, most people tend to go for options 3 or 4—they are prepared to make some sacrifices to buy a better-quality home. Next would probably be 1, then 2.

Some do borrow the maximum a lender will offer. Generally, lenders aren't silly and they won't lend you money that they don't believe you will be able to meet the repayments on. But it shouldn't be your preferred option.

Sometimes, it will make sense to go near the maximum lender limits. Perhaps if you've only been in the workforce for a few years and you're certain your salary will increase in leaps and bounds in the coming years. For example, if you're currently on $50 000, but believe your career path should see you earning $100 000 in a few years, then it *might* be worth taking out a higher mortgage now. But gambling on future pay rises is taking a big risk and you need to understand that. If the pay rises don't occur, you could be in for a long, difficult ride on that mortgage.

Deposits—how much do I need?

Wouldn't it be great if you could slap down $650 000 cash to purchase the average property in Australia?

Even if you could save your way to a house, would you? How long would it take you to save that much money? Answer: It doesn't matter. By the time you were able to save $650 000, the average house would probably be worth multiples of that sum—maybe $1–2 million.

How much of a deposit you will achieve will depend on your patience. And also what costs you're prepared to wear.

The 'cheapest' way to get into a property is by saving a 20 per cent deposit, plus legal costs (predominantly stamp duty). If you have that much money, you won't have to pay lender's mortgage insurance, or LMI, which is charged on loans where the borrower doesn't have enough to cover the 20 per cent plus legal costs. (I tackle LMI in chapter 7.)

Stamp duty and first-home owner grants

In chapter 3, I raise the 'myth of the 10 per cent deposit'. Why is it a myth? Because if you're buying a $600 000 home and you have $60 000 in savings, you don't necessarily have a 10 per cent deposit. You've forgotten stamp duty.

The good news for first-home buyers is that state governments (who charge stamp duty) usually go easier on you. In many cases, you won't be charged anything at all. Sometimes, when they do charge stamp duty, the blow might be softened with a government grant. Further, in some states, there are even more grants available if you're buying a brand-new home.

The differing state rules are too complex to go into here. If you're interested in roughly what those fees and grants could look like for your situation, go to www.brucebrammallfinancial.com.au and find the stamp duty calculator. You need to make a few simple choices and the stamp duty and government grants will be automatically calculated for you. (For even more information, search for *stamp duty* on the website of the state revenue office in your state.)

How different is it between states? Here's an example. If you buy a $600 000 newly constructed first home in Queensland, you will pay $0 in stamp duty, but $821.40 in other government fees. However, you'll get a $15 000 grant for the new property, so you're ahead more than $14 000.

The same scenario in the ACT will see government fees and charges of $21 155 and a government grant of $12 500, meaning you're down more than $8000.

If you can save 20 per cent plus your legals (taking into account first-home buyer discounts and grants), great. On a $500 000 home, that is going to require you to have somewhere between about $95 000 and $115 000, depending on what sort of property you buy and in which state (find the stamp duty calculator at www.brucebrammallfinancial.com.au).

For many first-home buyers, saving that amount would take too long. The cost of this impatience is generally lender's mortgage insurance. And most people pay LMI in order to get into their home sooner, rather than watch house prices rise further.

For example, let's take a couple who are buying their first home for $500 000. They need a loan for $450 000 to purchase their home, which would take them to a loan-to-valuation ratio of 90 per cent (LVR = $450 000/$500 000 = 90 per cent).

The LMI they are likely to have to pay on this loan is about $9000. That sounds like a lot. But there is another way of looking at it. Let's say it would take them another 12 months to save the extra $50 000 they would need to escape having to pay LMI, but in that time, the equivalent house has risen in value by 5 per cent to $525 000.

Not paying $9000 in LMI in this instance has cost them another $25 000 (plus they would have to save another $5000 to have 20 per cent of $525 000). If house prices are really moving, the house might have risen to $550 000 or more.

Where it would make sense to hold off on the purchase and continue to save would be if house prices were likely to stay flat, or even fall. Most first-home buyers won't have the knowledge to be able to confidently make that prediction. (I don't think too many property professionals really have the skills to do it either.)

Saving the 20 per cent plus legals

I do see a lot of clients who are buying their first homes who do have more than the 20 per cent plus legals required to purchase their home without paying lender's mortgage insurance. And it's wonderful to see them be able to escape paying lender's mortgage insurance.

In some cases, the deposit is a result of pure savings—and sometimes it is as a result of a fear of committing.

One couple I know had saved hard. They ended up saving for a decade, because they just couldn't commit to a mortgage. Between the roughly three- and ten-year mark, house prices doubled.

While they are happy with their eventual purchase, they understand they probably did themselves a disservice in waiting so long. Had they

(continued)

> ### Saving the 20 per cent plus legals *(cont'd)*
>
> gone ahead and purchased a smaller home when they had, say, $80000, they would have benefited from house prices doubling and had far greater equity to take into their second home—the one they eventually bought.
>
> The costs involved in *stepping stone* property are the first lot of stamp duty and the cost of selling that first property. But in many cases that will be dwarfed by the equity that they would have taken to the new home.

The first-home owner's first home loan

What are the major differences for first-home buyers getting their first home loan? There are a few things that you should particularly keep in mind.

Cheapest isn't necessarily best

You've never seen a debt like this before! It's enormous. But I can tell you that it's unlikely to be your biggest debt—that may well come with your second or third house. The temptation can be to go with the cheapest interest rate you can find. 'It's just someone else's money that I'm renting, isn't it? The cheaper the better!'

Have a refresher on what's important in a loan in chapter 4. If the cheapest loan is only a tiny amount (say, less than 0.1 per cent) more expensive than a product that has some other features you might get some financial value out of, then the cheapest home loan might not be the best for you.

And if this is going to be the first of many properties for you (homes plus investment properties), you might wish to start with a lender who will be able to go on the whole journey with you, as you move to create wealth over a long period of time.

Super cheap no-frills home loans certainly are the right product for some. But before rushing in to try to save a few dollars a week, make your decisions in the right order.

Paperwork for the bank

What's different for a first-home buyer when it comes to the paperwork required for their first bank loan? Officially, not much. See chapter 3 for the paperwork required by lenders.

But there are some subtle differences.

For example, you obviously won't have six months' worth of current loan statements. You should probably fill in the first-home owner grant paperwork (you're generally best to do this when you're filling out your loan application).

And you will need evidence of *5 per cent genuine savings*. Most banks want proof that you have got a minimum 5 per cent deposit for the purchase of the house. You will need to show them bank statements for three or six months to show that you have saved the money yourself. If they see a large gift in those savings, it can raise flags. While gifts are fine, banks usually want to see that you've received a gift and haven't spent it for three or six months. If you are going to receive a gift, it's better to get it earlier so that it can sit in your account for a period of months, or you might need a letter of explanation to the bank, saying that it is a non-repayable sum from the giver.

Don't fall overboard

Buying a home is pretty intense. But don't get pressured into doing something too fast. An extra few weeks, or months, won't make that big a difference. With your first home, we're talking big bucks. It's many, many multiples of your salary. So the dollars at stake are real.

Don't panic if you start to see some of the following warning signs, but make sure you hit the pause button and find someone to speak to, to get some advice if:

- your loan-to-valuation ratio is more than 90 per cent
- you have concerns about being able to meet the repayments
- you're being pressured to 'sign quickly, or the special deal is off'
- the bank's fees and charges are high, don't make sense, or haven't been fully explained to you
- it's all happened too quickly; you had just started considering buying a home and all of a sudden you're signing up for a mortgage.

If you're doing more than one of these, or are being pressured to do so by someone, get advice from someone independent.

The thrill of the chase

Every property market is different. In some states, Saturdays are a mad rush through homes that are open for inspection. Most sales in Australia are private sales, but in some markets there is a healthy mix of auctions also. See chapter 8 for more details on the differences between private sales and auctions.

But finding your dream home is generally exciting. You get to check out what you like and don't like in a home, make decisions as to what you will do in your own place, get some interior decorating ideas. And you will spend a lot of time getting into and out of cars.

When speaking with real estate agents, don't give away too much personal information. Don't give away your true budget, for example. If you end up negotiating with an agent and they know that you've got a certain amount to spend on a home, it will give them incentive to push you higher. If you feel like you have to tell them anything, then keep it a little lower than what you really have at your disposal.

But suck all of the information that you can out of them. If it's an existing home that is being sold, ask:

- why the buyer is selling
- if the current place is tenanted (it's usually pretty obvious)
- whether there have been any recent offers
- when renovations were done
- what amenities, schools and so on are close by (these will often be detailed on a printed flyer).

Take a notepad and make notes. It can get confusing when you've been to see so many properties. Later on, when places that you liked have sold, mark the prices in your notebook so that you can keep a track of comparable prices in the area.

Building equity in your home

(We're jumping ahead here to after the purchase. I cover structuring the purchase of property in chapter 7. And in chapter 8, I cover what's involved in purchasing your property.)

I've got to make sure something is very clear. Your home is not an investment.

Many people look at their home and think that 'it's a good investment'. Sure, it will probably end up appreciating in value over time, but your foremost concern in buying your home should not be its investment potential. The primary reason for buying your home should have been emotional—the sorts of things I outlined earlier in this chapter.

It's not an investment, primarily for two reasons. The first is that it will never generate any income for you. The second is that if you eventually want to upgrade, you will usually need to take the equity with you to reduce the loan on your new home. There are other reasons and we will cover those soon.

However...

Your home is an investment to the extent that you will develop equity in the home over time.

Equity in a home is developed in three ways. The first—and the one you have the most control over—is by paying down the home loan. If you take out a $400 000 loan and you pay it down to $350 000, then you have increased your equity by $50 000 (assuming its value doesn't fall). The second way is by the value of the home increasing. This tends to be a far faster, though less predictable, way of increasing equity. You might find that it takes you, say, five years to pay down your loan by even $50 000, but over the same five years, the value of your home might have increased from $500 000 to $640 000 (a 28 per cent increase). Combining both of these actions, your equity has grown from $100 000 to $290 000, but nearly three-quarters of the increase is as a result of the property improving in value. A third way is home improvements, such as renovations, which need to either be paid for with cash or further borrowings.

For home buyers aspiring to become property owners, it's this concept of equity growth that will help you use your home to purchase other assets. I cover this in more detail in chapter 6.

Trading up—your second and third home

Some people do buy their first home and live there for decades. But, on average, your first home will be one of two or three homes you purchase in your lifetime.

Most of the time, when you purchase your second or third (or fourth, fifth or sixth) home, you will sell the existing home and take the equity with you.

Let me show you an example. You bought your first home for $300 000, with a mortgage of $270 000. About eight years later, you've paid down the mortgage to $210 000, while the value of your home has increased to approximately $445 000. Your initial equity of $30 000 has grown to $235 000.

You're trading up. If your current home is worth $445 000, then your next home (bigger yard, closer to schools for those kids you found in the cabbage patch a few years back) might need to be, say, $700 000.

Of your $235 000 equity, it's going to cost you about $15 000 in sales costs (see the text box below) and the stamp duty on the new place is going to be $30 000 (though it depends what state you're in). You have $190 000 in equity to move with you. Your new home loan is going to be $510 000—nearly double your first home loan! But there's a good chance that you've had some pay rises since then.

If you can't go that far, don't. Trading up to a $650 000 property instead would leave you with a mortgage of about $460 000.

Upsizing and downsizing—the costs of moving home

The two main impediments to trading up (upsizing) and trading down (downsizing) in Australia are stamp duty—there are fewer stamp duty savings for buying second and subsequent homes—and the cost of selling your home.

Roughly, allow about 2.5 per cent to 3.5 per cent to sell your home, for agent's fees and advertising costs. It could be higher or lower, depending on the norm in your marketplace.

A typical story—buying our second home

As previously stated, our first home was perfect for my wife and me at that stage of our lives. Pre-kids, it was about lifestyle and a hatred of travel time. In pre-smartphone days, I read newspapers on the train, but I still found it dead time. It has always been important to me to minimise work travel time.

But for our second house, it was a different stage of life with two kids under three. We couldn't afford a backyard in Richmond. We had two choices. We could broaden our skill set and go all Pumpkin and Honey Bunny from *Pulp Fiction* ('Everybody be cool! This is a robbery!'). Or we could move further out.

Our preferred suburbs were at the top end of our affordability range. We looked at each other and agreed that we'd bite the bullet, accept a bigger mortgage than we'd hoped to end up with, and stay a little closer to town. So, we ended up with a smaller block than we'd have liked (that's what happens the closer you get to the CBD), but many factors had influenced that decision and we knew we made the right choice, no matter how much the new mortgage hurt!

Priorities change. Your reasons for buying your first home will be different to the criteria used for your second, which commonly will include the kids. A third house, or a major renovation, might be to house teenagers. The final home could be a downsizer. After that, your kids might be sizing you up for a nursing home!

Should I turn my home into an investment property?

Oh! The number of clients I have counselled on this topic! It's a very popular wish. You loved the place so much that you bought it. And even though you have to or want to move now, you don't want to let go. 'It will be a great little rental.'

It can make sense to do this in some circumstances. But it largely won't make financial (or even emotional) sense, unless you had this in mind and set this up correctly at the start. If you're trying to do this as a 'sensible' financial decision, it's more complicated than you would think. But I'll also come back to the scenarios where it *can* make sense, at the end of this section.

In most cases, the best thing you could do for your finances would be to sell it, take the equity to reduce the mortgage on your *new* home ... then specifically buy an investment property after that.

But first, here's why it usually won't work.

For the sake of the following examples, we are going to use a consistent set of numbers. The house was bought ten years ago for $300 000 and is now worth $500 000. The initial home loan of $270 000 has been reduced to $180 000. Current equity, therefore, is around $320 000.

The deposit for the new house?

You've probably ploughed your spare cash into your home mortgage. Where is your deposit going to come from? If you're now turning it into a rental, you might have some money in the redraw and offset accounts. But do you have enough for the deposit on the new home? And are you aware of the tax implications of taking money out of the redraw? (See more on this in chapter 7.)

Your new home loan is going to be huge!

There is $320 000 of equity sitting in your current home. If you don't sell and take that equity to your new home, the new loan (which is not tax-deductible) is going to be roughly $300 000 (allowing for some sale costs) higher than it could be.

Deductible and non-deductible debt isn't well structured

Sure, you'll have some investment debt, as well as a home loan on the new place. But your (deductible) investment debt is going to be small and your (non-deductible) home loan is going to be high. Pardon me, but that's arse about.

You can take 'profits' CGT free

One of the main benefits of a home over an investment property is that there is no capital gains tax on the *principal place of residence*, aka your home. If you sell when it has only ever been your home, profits are tax-free. If you convert it to a rental, any gains will be proportionately taxed according to how long it was a home versus an investment property.

Positively geared and paying tax

Because of the low debt, there's a good chance the property will be positively geared. If it is now rented out at $1667 a month ($20 000 a year), you might have to pay tax on the net income (still while you're getting no tax breaks on your higher debt for the new home).

You didn't buy the house as an investment

When you bought the house initially, it appealed to you. You didn't buy it with the sole intention of making money. If it was to be money-making, you should have used a different set of purchasing criteria (see chapter 6). And would you have bought this place? Usually, the answer will be no—you would have used different criteria, with more of an eye to capital growth.

You didn't set up the loans correctly

See more on this in chapters 4 and 7. If there was always a chance that you would turn this house into an investment property, then you should have set this up properly from the start, with an offset account. From a tax perspective, if you haven't done those things, they could be very costly errors at this point.

But it can make sense, if ...

There are times when you can turn your former home into an investment property and have it make some financial sense. And those are likely to include the following scenarios, or pre-planning:

- You have structured your loans correctly (see chapters 4 and 7, particularly in regards to offset accounts) and the tax-deductible debt will remain high.

- There isn't much equity in the current home, so there wouldn't be much equity to use to reduce the non-deductible loan at the new home.

- You have only lived there for, say, one year (perhaps to receive the benefits of first-home ownership, such as stamp duty concessions and first-home owner grants) and you were always intending to turn it into an investment property.

- You're moving interstate or overseas and you might move back into your home in a few years. This can mean saving on sale costs and new stamp duty when you move back into the home.

In figure 5.1, I show the difference between two options often considered by those thinking of keeping their first homes as investment properties. The first scenario shows what occurs when you keep your original home as an investment property. The second shows what happens when you sell your original home, purchase a new home (with minimal debt), then purchase an investment property with a debt structure optimised for investment purposes.

Figure 5.1: two scenarios—keeping your old home, and selling it and buying a new investment property

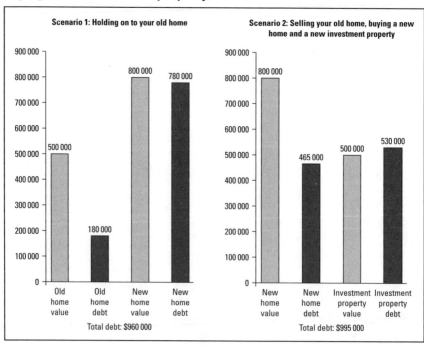

Decoding figure 5.1

In figure 5.1, scenario 2, we have assumed that you have decided to sell your original home (in scenario 1) and use that equity to purchase your new home, then to purchase an investment property, which you could then buy specifically for the purpose of making money.

Under this option, you have minimised the amount of non-deductible debt, in reducing the home loan on the new home from $780 000 to $465 000, while increasing the debt on your investment property from $180 000 to $530 000. That is, you have decreased your non-deductible debt by $315 000 and increased your investment (deductible) debt by $350 000.

Your total loans have increased by $35 000 (largely due to stamp duty), but due to the nature of tax deductions on the investment debt, it will actually be cheaper to service the slightly higher loan. And in the longer term, you will be able to pay your home loan down faster.

Homes versus investment properties—not the same game

There are so many differences between homes and investment properties (see the list in chapter 2). It's not just the 'emotional home purchase' versus the 'money-making investment property' concept that is important when you purchase. Really understanding the tax reasons is important.

Homes

A home is CGT free. If you live there, there will never be any tax to pay. If you're particularly blessed, you could buy it for $100 000, do nothing (or fix it up a little), and then sell it for $2 million a few years later and your tax bill will be, exactly, $0. Nada. Nothing.

But there are no tax deductions for anything you do to the house (except for things like a home office, which might then mean you incur CGT when you sell). You can't claim a deduction when something breaks or needs replacement. Neither are the costs of renovations, insurance, rates, water, gas or electricity deductible.

Investment properties

Virtually everything associated with an investment property is a tax deduction, including the interest on the loan and any repairs and maintenance. Also deductible are the costs of the managing agent, the rates, the service charges and insurances.

You can claim depreciation for all of the furnishings in the house (at various rates, determined by the Australian Tax Office). Also, for more recently built properties (those built after 1987), you can claim 2.5 per cent of the cost of the building itself (known as the *special building write-off*).

But you do have to pay CGT. CGT rules have changed over the years, but for assets bought after 21 September 1999, you get a 50 per cent discount if you have owned the asset for longer than 12 months before sale.

Property purchasing principles

It's huge. It's gigantic. As a result, when you take out your first home loan, you're usually a little shell-shocked for a period, as you wonder how you're going to deal with it. You will. (Well, nearly all of you will. Despite the best of intentions and efforts, some people will fall on hard times and will lose their homes.)

The reason it's so tough? Generally, it's because you have taken on the biggest financial commitment of your life. And you've got to make that commitment with no help in the form of tax breaks.

And just to ram it home ... here are the key points to take away from this chapter.

- Buying a home should be about lifestyle considerations — after all, you are going to live there.
- While renting is cheaper in the short and medium term, home ownership is the cornerstone of long-term wealth creation.
- Once you sort out why you're going to buy your home, you have to determine what to buy, and where.

- How far you are willing to go into debt when buying your house depends on a number of factors, including your stomach for risk.

- Obviously, with deposits, the bigger the better, but not if the time you'd spend saving up coincides with strong rises in property prices.

- First-home buyers have to consider that the cheapest interest rate does not necessarily equal the best possible loan. There are other important loan structure decisions that you need to carefully consider.

- Looking for a home is fun, but don't lose your head—ask lots of questions and take lots of notes.

- Homes are not investments, but you will generally develop equity in them, either through paying down the loan, the increasing value of the home, or through the improvements you make on them.

- When moving on to your second and third homes, your needs will be slightly different and you should factor these in.

- First homes can become investment properties, but in most cases it doesn't make sense to do so.

- In a tax sense, homes and investment properties are very different.

And that leads us to chapter 6.

6

Investment property — building your wealth

Now for a complete change of pace.

For this chapter, leave your emotions at the door.

I will not tolerate any sentimentality in this chapter. Only unemotional, unfeeling automatons allowed. There will be no 'I love it SOOOO much! Honey, let's get this one!'

Crying is banned. I won't be allowing you any tantrums at missed auctions, there will be no butterflies about it the night before and, certainly, if you think you can do this with a view to doing something nice for the world, then put this book down and go find a tree to hug.

Airy-fairy, like it or don't like it, 'could see us snuggling up on the couch, which would go here, watching the TV over there'...there'll be none of that crap in *this* chapter. Okay?

I'm going to get a little hard-arsed. Homes and investment properties *are* very, very different.

While a home needs to be cuddly and warm and safe and a place you're comfortable to hang around and bring friends and family and have lovely Christmases and birthday parties for the kids...an investment property needs to be none of those things to you. Why? *Because you're never going to live there.* So what does it matter?

An investment property is about one thing only.

Making money.

So, if you're not reading this to make money, then off you go. Find a tree. Give it a hug.

Sure, you might not always make money with investment property — this is not a guaranteed money-making investment. But making money is the *aim* of the game. And if you're not trying to do that, then it's not an investment property. And you're definitely doing it wrong.

You need money to make money...

True. Buying an investment property without having any money can prove tricky. But there are various ways of doing that. And getting the funding right is crucial to giving yourself the best chance of making your investment property work to help you grow wealth for your future.

As you might be used to hearing me say by now, investment properties are, in many ways, the opposite of homes. And the way they are funded goes along with that storyline.

With a home loan, arguably, the bigger the savings you put towards it, the better. With an investment property, the best way to fund it is often with none of your own savings. You read that right. None.

While you might aim for a deposit for your home of a minimum of 10 to 20 per cent, an investment property is best funded, from a tax perspective, by borrowing the lot (and a little more). If the investment property is $450 000, you borrow the whole $450 000, plus the stamp duties and legals (say $25 000) for a loan of $475 000.

Does that make sense? To many, that probably defies logic. 'Why would a bank lend more than the cost of a property to buy a property? Wouldn't that lead to a horrendous lender's mortgage insurance bill?'

The answer to the first is: This is no problem for a bank *if they have adequate security for their loan.* To the second: Possibly not a cent of lender's mortgage insurance.

Do you have adequate security? The answer hinges on your answer to this question: Do you own other property, and, if yes, how much equity do you have in it?

If you have sufficient equity in your own home (or other properties), then you might be able to purchase your investment property by borrowing everything. And if that's you, then you are in a position to fund an investment property in the most tax-efficient way.

However, let's not get too far ahead. You don't need to own your own home and have loads of equity in it to buy an investment property. It helps. But you can buy property in other ways. And the less of your own money you use, the better.

But let's step back for a minute.

Why is funding investment properties different?

In a word, tax.

The main difference between the debt for buying a home and buying an investment property is that the debt associated with an investment is a tax deduction, while a home mortgage is not. What makes a debt tax-deductible? If the debt is being used to generate income that is taxable, which includes rent, then the interest component of the mortgage repayments is deductible.

Tax deductibility changes the net cost of a debt enormously. Here's how. Let's compare a debt for $400 000 for Pat and Susie. They both earn $75 000 a year. Interest rates are at 6.5 per cent. We'll assume interest-only. And their marginal tax rate is 34.5 per cent (including 2 per cent for the Medicare levy).

Pat uses the debt to buy a home. The interest cost is $26 000. Because there's no tax deduction:

- Pat needs to earn $39 695 before tax to be able to pay the debt
- after tax, Pat needs to find $26 000 to pay the debt.

Susie buys an investment property. Her interest bill is also $26 000. However, given the tax deductibility and her income, she will get a tax return of $8970. This means:

- Susie will need to earn $26 000 before tax to be able to pay the debt
- after receiving her tax return, the net cost for Susie is $17 030.

No equity—starting with savings

You don't have to already have equity in property to buy an investment property (but it helps). If you don't, then you can still buy property the 'normal' way—that is, by using savings to fund the deposit. In some ways, this makes it more like buying a home (as in chapter 5), but with a few important differences.

The first is that state governments do not provide stamp duty relief (or, obviously, first-home owner grants) for investment property.

The second is the fact that the higher your investment debt, the bigger your tax deduction on the interest. So why wouldn't you borrow as much as you could for an investment property and use as little of your own as you needed to? If you borrowed 90 per cent of the cost of a property, you would be up for lender's mortgage insurance (see chapter 7 for more on that), but even the cost of the LMI is a tax deduction (or the interest on it is).

If you could choose your debt structure ...

If you could choose the way your debt was structured, you would choose to have all debt as tax-deductible.

Let's look at $1 million of debt. Often, that might be just a family home and one investment property. (Those looking to build bigger property investment portfolios might need debt in the millions of dollars.)

Here are three scenarios, all with $1 million worth of debt. The difference is the mix between what proportion is for a home (non-deductible) and which proportion is for an investment (deductible). (Again, in this example, we are excluding rental income for simplicity.)

We're going to use someone on the 39 per cent marginal tax rate (someone earning between $80 000 and $180 000 a year). The interest rate on all three scenarios is 6.5 per cent.

Scenario 1: All non-deductible debt

If you have $1 million worth of non-deductible debt, as in figure 6.1, then the cost of servicing that debt (interest-only) will be $65 000.

Figure 6.1: all debt non-deductible

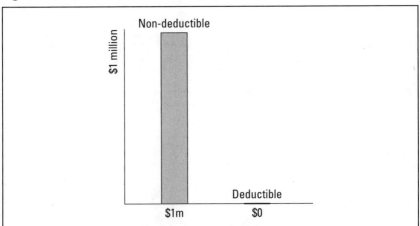

Scenario 2: Half non-deductible, half deductible

If you have $500 000 worth each of non-deductible and deductible debt, your interest bill is still $65 000, but you are going to get a tax deduction on half of it, reducing the net interest cost to $52 325, thanks to a tax return of $12 675, as shown in figure 6.2.

Figure 6.2: half deductible, half non-deductible

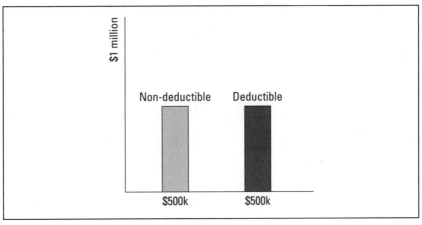

Scenario 3: All deductible debt

All of the interest on the $1 million of debt is tax-deductible. The total cost of $65 000 is reduced to a net cost of $39 650, thanks to a tax return of $25 350, as shown in figure 6.3.

Figure 6.3: all debt deductible

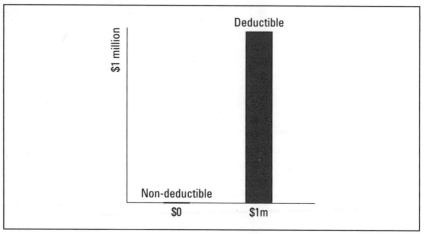

The point is that deductible debt is cheaper.

The only exception to that rule would be if there was a significantly higher interest rate charged on the investment debt, which is usually not the case when a residential property is the security. Banks often charge higher rates of interest for lines of credit, but it is usually a fairly small amount and would not change this equation considerably.

Buying an investment property before buying a home

Many people want to buy an investment property before buying a home, but will buy a home fairly soon. This included me.

The conundrum is this: If you buy an investment property first, you might not be eligible for first-home owner grants, or stamp duty concessions, when you later buy your home.

These issues need to be weighed up. Some states' schemes are incredibly generous to first-home buyers, while other states are, well, so-so. And because the schemes differ by state and there are so many variables, which are regularly being changed, unfortunately I can't give specific guidance in this book. You should check your own circumstances on the stamp duty calculator at www.brucebrammallfinancial.com.au.

It can still be worthwhile buying the investment property first in some circumstances.

Though it was many moons ago, it worked well for me. I bought my first investment property in January 2000. The first of the first-home owner grants (FHOGs) was to start in July that year. I weighed up whether it would be worthwhile holding off to buy a home first, then buy an investment property, in order to get the then $7000 grant. I wasn't sure how long it would take us to buy our first home, so after consideration, I decided to buy an investment property.

In March 2001, we bought our first home, in joint names, which meant we could not receive the then $7000 FHOG, because I had already purchased a property. (Had we bought the property in just Mrs DebtMan's name, then we would have been eligible for the grant.)

Do I regret not buying a home first? No. The grant was $7000. But over the course of the extra 14 months it took us to save for our home, the investment property had risen in value from $141 000 to the bank's valuation of $170 000. The extra equity was certainly worth more than the $7000 grant. As a bonus, it also reduced the lender's mortgage insurance we had to pay on our home.

There's no right or wrong answer here. Look into your state's offers on FHOG and stamp duty concessions as a starting point. Don't just automatically think 'I want the free government money'. For instance, if you don't want to buy a home for two to three years, but you want to buy an investment property now, weigh up your options.

There is also another possible solution—consider purchasing the investment property in one partner's name only. Later, purchase the *home* in the other partner's name. If the partner buying the home has not owned a property before, they should still get the FHOG and stamp duty concessions. Be aware of the risk you are running in this instance—how solid is your relationship? It's a serious question and some consideration should be given to this before entering this sort of arrangement. Seek legal advice in this situation.

If you decide to purchase an investment property first, here is a general rule to follow: while keeping in mind the costs of lender's mortgage insurance, minimise the amount of your own savings that you use for your deposit for the investment property and instead save your funds for your future home.

The cost of doing this will be extra LMI (and, as already covered, potentially lost stamp duty and first-home buyer grants). See table 7.2 (p. 157) for an example of the exponential charging rate of LMI.

For the moment, let's assume the following facts. You want to buy an investment property for $400 000 immediately and a home worth $500 000 in two to three years' time. You have $100 000 in savings now, and believe over the next two years you can save another $80 000.

You decide to get a loan for 89 per cent of the purchase price, or $356 000 (we'll assume stamp duties of $13 000). Your LMI will be about $5400.

What are you weighing up? Your option is to pay the LMI, or put in another $36 000 to reduce the loan to 80 per cent. If you keep the $36 000 in your own name, not using it as a deposit, it will be there for you to grow and use for your own home purchase in a couple of years.

(And, in the meantime, if you structure the loan to best effect—using interest-only with an offset account—you could use the $36 000 plus other savings to offset the interest on this loan until such time as you are ready to purchase your own home. See chapter 4 for more information on the power of offset accounts and chapter 7 for more on this specific strategy.)

Having equity in your own home (or any property)

The real power of property kicks in when you've got equity in property that you already own. Sounds a bit cruel, doesn't it—that you've got to have equity to create equity. But there's a good reason for it.

When a bank is lending hundreds of thousands of dollars to an individual, they want security. Understandably. And the best security (from a bank's perspective) if you want to buy bricks and mortar is more bricks and mortar.

If you have considerable equity in another property, then a bank will feel comfortable lending you lots more. Banks love property as security—better than even the best blue-chip shares.

Banks will comfortably (and largely happily) lend you up to 80 per cent of the value of a property—without requiring lender's mortgage insurance—so long as you have enough income to service the loan. (They will actually lend you more, but then you get into LMI territory and it gets a little more complex, so we'll deal with a situation of less than 80 per cent for now.)

Therefore ... if you have a home (or several properties) worth $1 million, a bank will happily lend you up to $800 000.

So, now we're returning to the questions from the start of this chapter ... if you have equity in your home, banks will be far more likely to lend you enough money to purchase investment properties, without having to use your savings. Here's a realistic example to show how this works.

Example

Steven and Jamie bought their home seven years ago. It's now worth $800 000 and their home loan is $250 000. They believe they can afford a $500 000 investment property.

They want a loan for the entire purchase price, plus costs (stamp duty, and so on), totalling approximately $530 000. They have a rental appraisal from a real estate agent suggesting the house should rent for $390 a week ($20 280 a year).

This would leave them with an application to a bank with properties worth a total of $1.3 million, with loans of a total of $780 000.

What's the bank's thinking process? Pretty much this: 'Okay, incomes are a tick. Rent is fine. We'd have $780 000 of debt on $1 300 000 million of property. The debt would be 60 per cent of the combined value of the properties (an LVR of 60 per cent). Comfortable with that. Approved.'

This is a typical scenario of how a loan for more than 100 per cent of the value of an investment property would be approved. Why? Because the bank would take *security* over both the home and the investment property. (How that security is offered involves some choice for Steven and Jamie, which I cover in chapter 7).

Of course, it's not quite that simple—there are other boxes to tick. But so long as Steven and Jamie have reasonable credit records and their expenses aren't batting out of the ballpark on a normality scale (Are they agisting five horses? Sponsoring 32 children in Africa? Financially supporting their own parents? Do they have nine children of their own?), they are likely to be approved.

Having equity in other real estate gives banks the security to lend to you without you having to put up cash to fund deposits. And if you don't have to put up your own cash, you can leave it in the offset or redraw account for your own home loan, saving you interest on a non-deductible debt.

Equity—a good problem to have

Having equity in a property is a good problem to have—in fact, it is ultimately the most important part of owning property (the other major one being the income stream for investors).

Accessing equity is often frowned on. Rightly so, if equity is used to purchase consumables or depreciating assets, such as cars or holidays.

But it's not bad if it's accessed to purchase quality investment assets. You are using equity developed in property to try to create greater wealth for you and your family. It's not being spent frivolously.

Bank property valuations—the only ones that matter

Who determines the value of your home or investment property? Ultimately, you and a buyer or seller—it can really only be determined when you agree on a price and a property is sold.

But any time a bank is offering a loan over a property, they will need to value it.

Banks use property valuation companies to assess a property's value. Valuers compare the subject property to others in the area that have recently sold.

When it comes to lending, the bank's valuation is the only one that matters. They won't care what your council rates say, or what you think it's worth. Though sometimes you can argue the point and occasionally have a win.

If you are looking to borrow money against a property, depending on the banking package you have chosen, your bank will often pay for a valuation for you (though they might not tell you what the valuation found). Many professional packages (see chapter 4 for more on pro-packs) will include occasional free valuations on your property, if required, and can be another reason to take a professional package with a bank. However, you may have to pay a few hundred dollars for a valuation.

Valuations done for banks are generally fairly conservative with the estimated price they place on a property. This is understandable, in that the bank needs to know, essentially, the minimum they could get for a property in a tough market, in case that's about to occur.

But sometimes bank valuations are just patently wrong and need to be challenged.

A client of mine was looking to upgrade his home and needed a new loan. He believed his flat was worth approximately $450 000, and his rates notice said $420 000.

The first valuation from a bank came in at $350 000. He was shocked. He gathered some evidence from nearby sales and the information, which suggested it was worth at least $400 000, was passed back to the valuer. A new valuation came back at $375 000. But still, the customer couldn't believe the valuers were right.

So, another bank was used. That second bank used a different valuation firm, which then valued his home at $410 000. It wasn't the $450 000 that he thought it was worth, but at least the property was now valued at an amount that would allow him to complete his plans.

Maximising investment property loans

With a home loan, the great struggle is to pay it off. From the day you get your home loan, you're constantly aware of it being there and you're also constantly battling to pay it down, while maintaining a semblance of a lifestyle.

How you treat a loan for an investment property should be different.

Essentially, you should probably aim to never pay it off. That's right. In many, even most, circumstances, paying down or paying off your investment property home loan should be a case of *never, not interested* and *have other priorities*.

Why? Because the debt on an investment property is a tax deduction. And if you've got other non-deductible debt elsewhere, such as your home loan, then paying off your investment property debt should be down the list of priorities. If you have both home and investment property debt, all spare cash should be focused on paying down the home loan.

Using interest-only

Banks do understand this. They understand that for your personal taxation purposes, it makes sense not to pay down the principal of the loan when it's for investment purposes.

That is, each month and year, you only pay the interest on the loan. The principal remains the same, year in and year out. You take out a $350 000 interest-only loan and at the end of the third year, the principal owing on the property is still $350 000.

How is this better? If you had a loan of $500 000 at 6 per cent interest-only, the annual interest charge is going to be $30 000. However, if you borrowed $500 000 at 6 per cent on a principal and interest loan over 30 years, your repayments are going to be more like $35 973. That extra $5973 (each year) would be far better being used to pay down your own home loan.

And this compounds over many years.

Interest-only's downside — but I have the solution!

Banks do eventually want the principal repaid. They tend to only allow interest-only loans for given periods, often up to 10 years.

There is a downside to making a loan interest-only for an extended period. And that is, when the loan term finishes its interest-only period, it will revert to principal and interest. And that will lead to higher

---

repayments, because you have a shorter time frame to repay the principal of the loan.

For example, interest-only repayments on a $500 000 loan are going to be $2500 a month, where principal and interest over 30 years would be $2998 a month and over 20 years (if you took the first 10 years as interest-only) would be $3582 a month.

I come armed with solutions. In most cases, you will be able to either renegotiate the loan with your provider, or take your business to another bank and start a new interest-only loan.

Renegotiating can become a problem as you age. If you're on the other side of 60, for example, it could be harder to refinance to another lender, who would have to take into account your ability to repay the loan.

When should I do P&I on an investment?

Making principal and interest repayment on your investment property isn't wrong—not at any time. It's just generally not as tax efficient as paying interest-only.

Repaying P&I on loans can be the right choice when you wish to pay down the principal to increase your equity, or where you don't have any non-deductible debt (particularly a home loan) to repay.

Structuring your loan—an introduction

As discussed earlier, it is possible to borrow more than the full value of the investment property. Banks will give you a loan, for example, of potentially $530 000 for a property worth $500 000.

But they want security. If they're going to lend you more than the value of the property you're buying, they're generally going to want further properties as security.

If your home is worth $600 000 and you only have a $100 000 loan on it, then a bank can see a lot of equity that they could potentially accept as security on the new investment property that you've got your eye on, valued at $500 000.

In table 6.1 you can see that the total loans are well below the 80 per cent figure at which lender's mortgage insurance might be payable, so (subject to other things being 'normal') the bank would usually approve this loan.

Table 6.1: loan-to-valuation ratios on combined home and investment property loans

	Loan	Property value	Loan-to-valuation ratio (LVR)
Home	$100 000	$600 000	17%
Investment property	$530 000	$500 000	106%
Total	$630 000	$1 100 000	57%

What becomes important is how you structure the loan. I go into more detail on this in chapter 7, but let me raise an important point here.

A bank will always aim to maintain the maximum security it can. So, as a general rule, if you walk into a bank to get the above loan, they will often say that the 'easiest' way to secure this loan is to put both properties up as security against both of the loans. 'That sounds okay,' you think. But beware.

This is known as *cross-collateralisation* of the properties. You have two properties worth $1.1 million and you put both properties up jointly as security for the loan. Banks love this. And this is generally what they'd recommend. There would be just two loans, which makes things simple.

However, there is another option and it's usually safer to protect your most important asset—your home. If everything turns pear-shaped—you lose your job, your relationship breaks down, you're unable to work through illness—you would still want to hold on to your home, wouldn't you? With cross-collateralisation, banks can (and possibly would) sell both properties to satisfy your debts.

One way of achieving greater protection for yourself—more on this in chapter 7—would be to have two loans for the investment property purchase. Put 80 per cent of the loan required against the investment property, with the remainder against your own home. This will usually mean you have three loans, structured like table 6.2.

Table 6.2: protective unbundled loans

Security	Loan	Property value	LVR
Home	$100 000	$600 000	17%
Home (investment property loan)	$130 000		26%
Investment property	$400 000	$500 000	80%
Total	$630 000	$1 100 000	57%

By doing this, you are reducing the bank's security over the investment property to 80 per cent and have greater protection for your main asset, the family home.

Creating real wealth—building a property portfolio

One investment property won't make you rich. It will, over time, probably improve your lifestyle, either by increasing your income (as it turns from negatively to positively geared), or your overall wealth (via increased equity). But it won't make you rich.

Sorry to say this, but two properties probably won't either.

Building real wealth through property investment requires determination and a time period of more than a decade, the purchase of a number of properties and, inevitably, a mountain of debt. That is, you are combining wealth's two great power tools—compounding growth and leverage.

If a property portfolio is your aim, then only you can decide how many it is that you require to build the wealth (be that capital or income) that you require. But here is how it's done.

Let's assume that three years ago, you bought your first investment property, using your home as security. At the time of purchase, your home was worth $600 000 and the investment property you bought was worth $400 000.

Over those three years, you've experienced average growth on your properties and average rents. For the purposes of this example, we're going to use growth of 5 per cent and rental returns of 4 per cent (a constant yield of 4 per cent of total property values), giving a total return from property of 9 per cent. For simplicity, we'll assume all loans are interest-only. Figure 6.4 (overleaf) shows how this will all shake out.

Figure 6.4: building a portfolio

Price growth: 5%
Rental: 4%
Stamp duty and purchase costs: 6%

	Year 0	Year 1	Year 2	Year 3	Year 4	Year 5	Year 6	Year 7
Home	$600 000	$630 000	$661 500	$694 575	$729 304	$765 769	$804 057	$844 260
Investment 1	$400 000	$420 000	$441 000	$463 050	$486 203	$510 513	$536 038	$562 840
Investment 2				$463 000	$486 150	$510 458	$535 980	$562 779
Investment 3						$510 000	$535 500	$562 275
Investment 4								$560 000
Investment 5								
Investment 6								
Value	$1 000 000	$1 050 000	$1 102 500	$1 620 625	$1 701 656	$2 296 739	$2 411 576	$3 092 155
Loans								
Home	$100 000	$100 000	$100 000	$100 000	$100 000	$100 000	$100 000	$100 000
Investment 1	$424 000	$424 000	$424 000	$424 000	$424 000	$424 000	$424 000	$424 000
Investment 2				$490 780	$490 780	$490 780	$490 780	$490 780
Investment 3						$540 600	$540 600	$540 600
Investment 4								$593 600
Investment 5								
Investment 6								
Total loans	$524 000	$524 000	$524 000	$1 014 780	$1 014 780	$1 555 380	$1 555 380	$2 148 980
Net equity	$476 000	$526 000	$578 500	$605 845	$686 876	$741 359	$856 196	$943 175
Rental income	$16 000	$16 800	$17 640	$37 042	$38 894	$61 239	$64 301	$89 916
Yield to debt	3.77%	3.96%	4.16%	4.05%	4.25%	4.21%	4.42%	4.39%

Year 8	Year 9	Year 10	Year 11	Year 15	Year 20	Year 25	Year 30
$886 473	$930 797	$977 337	$1 026 204	$1 247 357	$1 591 979	$2 031 813	$2 593 165
$590 982	$620 531	$651 558	$684 136	$831 571	$1 061 319	$1 354 542	$1 728 777
$590 918	$620 464	$651 487	$684 062	$831 481	$1 061 204	$1 354 396	$1 728 590
$590 389	$619 908	$650 904	$683 449	$830 736	$1 060 253	$1 353 182	$1 727 041
$588 000	$617 400	$648 270	$680 684	$827 375	$1 055 964	$1 347 707	$1 720 053
	$620 000	$651 000	$683 550	$830 859	$1 060 410	$1 353 382	$1 727 297
			$685 000	$832 622	$1 062 660	$1 356 253	$1 730 961
$3 246 763	$4 029 101	$4 230 556	$5 127 084	$6 232 002	$7 953 789	$10 151 275	$12 955 885
$100 000	$100 000	$100 000	$100 000	$100 000	$100 000	$100 000	$100 000
$424 000	$424 000	$424 000	$424 000	$424 000	$424 000	$424 000	$424 000
$490 780	$490 780	$490 780	$490 780	$490 780	$490 780	$490 780	$490 780
$540 600	$540 600	$540 600	$540 600	$540 600	$540 600	$540 600	$540 600
$593 600	$593 600	$593 600	$593 600	$593 600	$593 600	$593 600	$593 600
	$657 200	$657 200	$657 200	$657 200	$657 200	$657 200	$657 200
			$726 100	$726 100	$726 100	$726 100	$726 100
$2 148 980	$2 806 180	$2 806 180	$3 532 280	$3 532 280	$3 532 280	$3 532 280	$3 532 280
$1 097 783	$1 222 921	$1 424 376	$1 594 804	$2 699 722	$4 421 509	$6 618 995	$9 423 605
$94 412	$123 932	$130 129	$164 035	$199 386	$254 472	$324 778	$414 509
4.60%	4.58%	4.81%	4.78%	5.81%	7.41%	9.46%	12.08%

After your first purchase, you had two properties worth $1 million. At year three, they have grown in value to $1.157 million. A second investment property is bought for $463 000 — roughly the equivalent in value to the property purchased three years ago. The debt to go with the second investment property is approximately $491 000 (106 per cent).

Another two years later (year five), the portfolio (including home) has now grown in value to $1.787 million, with debt of $1.014 million. Then you buy another similar investment property for $510 000, with debt of $540 600.

In year seven, a fourth investment property is purchased for $560 000 (with debt of $593 600). Following this purchase, you now have properties worth $3.092 million, with debt of $2.149 million.

In years nine and eleven, you 'rinse and repeat'. You buy properties worth $620 000 and $685 000, with debts of $657 200 and $726 100 respectively.

Then you stop buying.

At this point, you have properties worth $5.127 million, with debts of $3.532 million, making equity of $1.594 million. Your rent roll has increased to $164 000 a year (equivalent to 4.78 per cent of your total debt).

What happens next?

In year 15, the value of your properties has grown to $6.232 million. The debt is still the same, at $3.532 million. Your net equity has now grown to $2.7 million. Rent has increased to $199 000, or 5.81 per cent of debt.

Move forward another five years, to year 20. The properties are worth $7.954 million, with debt of $3.532 million, providing equity of $4.421 million. Rent is $254 500, a yield versus your debt of 7.41 per cent.

At year 25, your properties are worth $10.151 million, with equity of $7.126 million, rent of $325 000 and a rent-to-debt yield of 9.46 per cent.

And ... when you've been at this for 30 years, your portfolio is worth $12.956 million, with equity of $9.424 million and rental income of $414 500 (a yield on debt of 12.1 per cent).

This is the power of property. Growth over time, in both equity and income, that can help ensure your financial future.

Note that this description is a simplistic depiction of growing a property portfolio and does not take into account a considerable number of costs and factors that would impact on cashflow, both up and down. These include depreciation, agent's fees, maintenance costs for the properties, land tax and insurances. But neither does it take into account that your debt could well have been considerably paid down as your income increases. Also, we have used a 5 per cent annual increase in the value of property prices. Property price rises DO NOT, sadly, rise uniformly in this way!

Diversifying your property portfolio

Anyone building a property portfolio such as the previous example needs to be aware of the rules of diversification. That is, having all of your property investments in one state, or city, can cause issues if that area is hit harder, financially, by what is happening in the broader economy.

For example, in the early 1990s, Victoria was known as the rustbucket state because of its heavy reliance on manufacturing. In 2012 to 2014, when the rest of the country's property was booming, Queensland was holding back because of state-based economic issues.

This can create opportunity over time. If growth in some states is held back because of economic or political factors, investment opportunities can present themselves. If you can see that a particular state's property is falling behind the national average growth rates, then it could provide an opportunity to invest in that market.

In 2014, for example, Queensland property prices had fallen well behind the growth rates of Sydney and Melbourne. According to real estate data at the time of writing, the median property price for Brisbane was $493 000, while for Sydney it was $795 000 and for Melbourne it was $683 000. That meant Sydney's property prices were nearly 61 per cent higher than Brisbane and Melbourne's were 39 per cent higher. Were Melbourne and Sydney overvalued? Was Brisbane undervalued? The answer could be a bit of both.

If you are building a portfolio, there will be a natural inclination to buy your first properties in the capital city of your state. But diversification is important and can actually help improve returns.

Coping with huge debt

In the examples where we have discussed growing a portfolio, we are talking about an investor taking on huge debt. Many people might look at the debt on the seven properties (home, plus six investments) and think: 'You've got to be kidding! There is no way a bank would lend me that much money. And even if they did, I couldn't sleep at night knowing that I owe that amount.'

That's an understandable concern. Owing $3.5 million to a bank, or to several banks, sounds scary. But understand that this is not something that you're doing overnight. You're not going from 0 to 100 km/h in 3.5 seconds, like a Formula One Ferrari. That debt is built over time, both as rental income grows and the equity in your properties grows.

If you are sure that property is your thing, then you will have to become comfortable with big debt built over time. Unless you are buying very cheap property such as flats, or properties in rural and regional areas (which I don't recommend—flats don't have much land associated with them and therefore have no scarcity value, while rural and regional properties have plenty of land, but no scarcity value), property purchases are done in lots of, generally, greater than $400 000, most of which will need to be funded by debt.

Take another look at the numbers in figure 6.4 (see p. 114). The debt is built over time, as rents are increasing, and as you are building equity. We are talking about a plan that is implemented over a dozen years, but the rewards are then enjoyed throughout the rest of your life.

Negative gearing explained

Negative gearing. Two words every bit as famous in Australia as Bondi Beach, Collingwood Magpies and Anzac Day. Known by even those who have absolutely no interest in investing.

But, depending on your point of view, negative gearing is either an investor's greatest ally, or a devil-child responsible for keeping property prices higher than they would otherwise be.

Negative gearing means that an investor is making a loss on an investment on a cash basis. In its simplest terms, it means something like the following has happened during the course of a financial year (which ends on 30 June each year):

- Rental income: $20 000

- Property expenses: $40 000 (including loan interest, agent's fees, insurance, rates and general maintenance)

- The investor has had to put in a further $20 000 of her own cash.

The *negative* is the $20 000 that the investor has had to cover. The *gearing* is that the largest part of the $40 000 of property expenses is likely to be the interest payable on the investment property loan.

In Australia, if you make a loss on an investment, you are allowed to claim that loss against your personal income tax. Therefore, if you earn $120 000 a year, you can claim that $20 000 loss against your income. With a marginal tax rate of 39 per cent (including the Medicare levy), it means that you would get $7800 of that $20 000 back, reducing your net loss to $12 200. (You might have further non-cash deductions, such as depreciation. Speak to your accountant for more information.)

Moving from negatively to positively geared

Negative gearing tends to occur in the early years of geared property investment ownership (that is, any property on which there are borrowings), particularly if the property has been predominantly or totally funded by debt. In most cases, if you have borrowed the entire purchase price of a property, you will be negatively geared.

Properties naturally move from negatively to positively geared over time, as two things occur. The most common is through rents increasing, which lifts your income. However, the interest component of the loan will decrease, if you are paying principal and interest also.

Negative gearing doesn't make sense on its own. It can only be a good strategy if the investment that you've purchased is increasing in value by more than what you're losing on a cash basis.

That is, if you're negatively geared by $20 000 (from which you might get back up to $9800 on the highest marginal tax rate, making a net loss of $10 200), then your property needs to be increasing by a multiple of the net loss each year.

If you have a $500 000 property and you're losing $10 200 a year, then if the property increases in value by 5 per cent each year, from $500 000 to $525 000, then the $10 000 loss might seem justified. (Properties will decrease in value some years, so we are talking about average growth rates.)

And over time, both rising rents and growth in the property's value will eventually mean that negative gearing turns positive, and the growth on the property is then a real reward. But, depending on the property, it can take a decade or so to reach this point.

The aim of most property purchases should be to get a mixture of growth both in underlying value and in the income (rent) being earned by the asset. Negative gearing is a great friend of investors. But it's constantly under the threat of attack, so be aware that it might not always exist for investors, if governments decide to end this arrangement.

Geared property in self-managed super funds (SMSFs)

If you hadn't noticed, there's an army of special investors growing in Australia. They are taking over the joint.

While SMSFs have been around for decades, interest in them has exploded in the last 10 to 15 years. As at mid 2014, there are now more than 528 000 SMSFs operating, with one million members. That's nearly 5 per cent of Australians being a member of an SMSF, and the growth suggests that it won't be slowing down any time soon.

SMSFs have always been able to invest in property. But prior to 2007, they were banned from borrowing to invest, except in very limited circumstances, which didn't include taking out property mortgages.

In 2007, the Australian Taxation Office changed the rules to allow SMSFs to borrow. It caught the entire industry by surprise — experts thought gearing would be further restricted, not opened wider. In 2010, the rules were updated. That is when the rules governing *limited recourse borrowing arrangements* (LRBAs—more on these later in this chapter) were born and SMSF gearing in property started to really take shape. (Search *LRBA* at www.brucebrammallfinancial.com.au for more information and articles on this topic.)

SMSFs can now borrow to invest directly in property—residential and commercial. But the rules are complex—it is not a straight replica of what can be done in the cases that are discussed elsewhere in this book. And, as such, I will only deal with this in a summarised form here.

Fundamentally, the issues are the same. You purchase a property with an amount of borrowings. You receive rent and potentially other tax advantages and aim to own the property for an extended period of time, as it slowly builds equity and great income (through rents rising).

But the actual mechanics are different.

Superannuation 101

First, you need to understand a little about superannuation. Superannuation is an investment vehicle, whereby the government gives tax concessions in order for Australians to save for their retirement.

The tax concessions mean that a complying superannuation fund is taxed at no more than 15 per cent on its income. Under certain circumstances, it will be taxed at just 10 per cent (for capital gains) or 0 per cent (for pension funds).

These rates compare with personal marginal tax rates as high as 49 per cent (in 2014). The benefits of investing inside super can be considerable. If you are receiving positive income of $10 000 from your property, the highest marginal tax payer in Australia will pay approximately $4900 in income tax on that income, where that same property owned in an SMSF would pay a maximum of $1500, and potentially $0.

The downside of investing in super is access. You can't get money out of super until you hit a *condition of release*. Depending on what year you were born, the main conditions of release are turning 55 and retiring (if you were born before mid 1960), turning 60 and changing jobs or retiring (for those born after mid 1964), or turning 65.

Property bought outside of super can be sold and the profits taken whenever you wish, though I strongly argue that property is a hold-till-you-die investment anyway.

Most people in Australia will have their super sitting with an APRA-regulated fund (industry, corporate, government or retail super funds). Those looking for more control over their super often choose SMSFs, where they take control of investing their superannuation.

Tax-free returns!

(The following is based on superannuation rules current at the time of writing. Governments have a habit of fiddling with superannuation rules and it's strongly recommended that readers speak with their advisers before investing in this area.)

To cut to the chase ... the real reason for investing in property (geared or ungeared) in an SMSF is the end game. The end game is when superannuation switches from being something in which you're building assets (accumulation mode) to something that is paying you an income (pension mode).

When a fund becomes a pension fund—which is required to pay a pension income—a super fund moves into a zero-tax environment. No tax on income earned in the fund. No tax on capital gains.

That's right.

Whatever income is being derived in the fund is earned tax-free. If you have a positively geared property in super, then no tax is paid on the net income the fund is receiving.

And no capital gains tax. If you bought a property for $500 000 in an SMSF and then you sell it ten years later for $1 000 000, there is no tax paid on the $500 000 gain. (This compares with tax rates of either 10 or 15 per cent for income and gains inside a super fund generally and up to 49 per cent in your personal name).

If you sold it for $5 000 000, there would be no tax to pay on your $4.5 million gain.

And if the person receiving the pension is aged over 60, they pay no tax on any income received from the pension.

Warning—SMSF gearing is not for property newbies

Anyone considering a geared property in an SMSF is strongly advised to see a financial adviser and/or mortgage broker who is experienced in the area.

Also, I don't believe SMSF property gearing is for property virgins. That is, don't buy a geared property in super, unless you have experience with property outside of super. The risks are higher and property investment is complex, because of the hands-on nature of property investment.

But for seasoned property investors who have a minimum of $200 000 in an SMSF, which can include combined balances for couples, then geared property inside an SMSF is something to consider.

How is property in SMSFs different?

By law, any property purchased inside an SMSF must be done under a certain structure.

Obviously, you need an SMSF. The governing document for an SMSF is a trust deed, which specifically needs to allow for geared property investment (which not all do).

The limited recourse borrowing arrangement rules state that the property must also be purchased inside a separate entity—broadly referred to as a *bare trust* or *holding trust*—which holds the asset on trust for the SMSF until the final instalment of the loan is paid. At this time, the bare trust may dissolve, or transfer the asset to the SMSF.

Lenders will generally insist on both the SMSF and the bare trust having *corporate trustees*. These are companies that are usually only used as a trustee for these two vehicles—do not use a company that has been used elsewhere, such as to run your family business. (Always seek professional advice in this area.)

SMSF property don'ts

SMSFs have some complex rules that we can't go into great detail on here. These include that an SMSF cannot purchase a residential property from a related party, that it can't use borrowings to improve an asset and that you can't actually use the property yourself—for example, your SMSF can't buy a holiday home that you intend to use occasionally.

An SMSF can, however, purchase a commercial property from a related party, such as a business owner operating their business out of a premises, which is a favourite of SMSF trustees.

The list of don'ts is too long to cover in any detail here. I strongly advise seeing an SMSF professional before you actively consider purchasing any property inside an SMSF.

Limited recourse borrowing arrangements—what does that mean?

The term *limited recourse* means the lender has a limited security for the loan. In the case of an SMSF, the security is limited to the investment property.

That is, if a lender has loaned $400 000 for a $500 000 property, they may only sell the property itself if the borrower fails to make repayments. If the property fell in value to $300 000, the lender can only get the sale price of the property—it can't go after the other assets of the super fund.

Banks now seek a personal guarantee from the trustees in regards to non-performing loans. That is, they may pursue the trustees as individuals and the other assets they hold outside of super in order to satisfy the loan.

Different LVRs

Because of the limited recourse nature of the loans—which increases the risk for the lender—banks usually restrict lending to SMSFs. Most banks will lend to approximately 70-80 per cent of the purchase price of the property. (This compares with lending potentially more than 100 per cent outside of super.)

Higher interest rates

Banks will usually also charge a higher interest rate, to cover them for the greater risks. At mid 2014, major banks were generally charging about 1 per cent higher than would be available for the same property for someone buying a property in their own name. This interest-rate premium has been reducing with competition.

You be the lender!

It is also possible for you to become the lender for your geared SMSF property purchase. If you have access to funds outside of super (either cash or sufficient equity in other properties), you could raise the funds necessary to become the lender to your SMSF. There is a considerable list of legal requirements that must be met—you can't just plonk the money into your SMSF and call it a loan.

For more information on this topic, search for the article entitled 'DIY and Property: You be the banker' at www.brucebrammallfinancial.com.au.

SMSF geared property—why would you?

The same basic principles apply as to why you would consider a property through an SMSF as an investment.

Gearing allows you to control a much larger asset. If the asset then grows in value, your returns are leveraged. (Similarly, if the asset falls in value, your losses are magnified.)

For example, take an SMSF with $250 000. If that super fund were to grow by 10 per cent over a period of time, the super fund would be worth $275 000.

Potentially, you could use approximately $130 000 as your deposit to cover the purchase of a $500 000 property. The $130 000 covers the 20 per cent deposit ($100 000) and the remainder would be used to cover stamp duty and other property purchase costs.

The super fund now has assets of $620 000 (a $500 000 property, plus $120 000 of other assets). If the assets in that super fund then increase by 10 per cent, the super fund would be worth $682 000, an increase of $62 000.

Negative gearing in SMSFs

One of the main similarities *and* differences between an SMSF and investing in your own name is the impact of negative gearing.

SMSFs do qualify for tax deductions for all of the same property costs that an individual can claim for. They can claim the cost of interest on loans, agent's fees, insurances, maintenance and rates.

The main difference is the tax rate in super is a maximum of 15 per cent. That means that if a property is negatively geared to the tune of $10 000 a year, an individual might get a tax return of up to $4900, reducing the cost to $5100, while a super fund will get a maximum return of $1500 (or $0 if the super fund is in pension).

The negative gearing associated with super property investments has a lesser value. This lower tax rate is often made up for, as mentioned earlier in this chapter, by the fact that the super fund won't pay any tax when it is in pension phase.

Strong warning—don't attempt this without help

A second warning—you will need a professional to guide you through the process, particularly if you have not invested in property before.

SMSFs are powerful investment vehicles for your retirement, but the penalties for getting it wrong can be catastrophic—the ATO can penalise trustees potentially hundreds of thousands of dollars for making major errors in an SMSF and can potentially tax the entire fund at as much as 45 per cent of its assets.

Property purchasing principles

One of the oldest debates in investing is the debate over which is better: shares or property. Shares people don't like the fact that property is so big and requires so much debt, while property people don't like the wild fluctuations that are inherent with shares, amongst many other arguments.

Personally, I'm an avid investor in both. A good diversified portfolio should have both, even if you're weighted more heavily towards one than the other. Property investors could use the increased liquidity that comes with shares for a portion of their portfolio and shares people would benefit from having assets that don't fluctuate so wildly.

If you think that property is probably your thing, make sure you do it properly. Too many people lose too much money because they buy awful property. Very briefly, in my opinion, avoid highrises, development property, anything too far from the major metropolitan capitals and anything that you're offered at a seminar run by a developer.

If you're wondering how the numbers would stack up in your situation, find yourself a good financial adviser and/or mortgage broker to go through the numbers.

And just to ram it home...here are the key points to take away from this chapter.

- Investment properties should be treated very differently from homes; it sometimes makes sense to borrow more than 100 per cent of the value of an investment property.

- Because the costs for investment properties are tax-deductible, the after-tax cost of the interest is lower.

- If you have some equity in your home, you have more and better options to structure your debt on your investment property.

- While buying an investment property prior to buying your first home can mean you can lose out on first-home buyer grants and stamp duty concessions, it can sometimes be worth it.

- If you have equity in your home or other property, banks will lend you over 100 per cent of the property value for an investment property by taking your existing property as security.

- Accessing equity in your home can be sensible if it's used to purchase investment assets.

- Bank valuations of property are always conservative, but they are the valuations that matter in calculating the size of the loans you can get.

- Paying off investment property loans often should not be a high priority when you also have a home loan.

- The benefits of interest-only loans are great, but interest-only loans do tend to have a sting in their tale, as they have shorter repayment periods of the principal when the interest-only term wears off. Luckily you can usually renegotiate another interest-only loan—if not with your existing bank, then with another one.

- If you don't have a home loan to pay off, it can make sense to pay principal and interest on your investment property loans.

- When you structure your loans, you can cross-collateralise your properties to maximise the size of loan you can get. But to protect your home, you may want to create a different loan structure to minimise the security against your home.

- Building real wealth through property investment requires a long time period, a number of properties and a mountain of debt but, structured right, with growth in equity and income, it can help ensure your financial future.

- It is best to have a diverse property portfolio, across different states and cities.

- If you are investing in property, you have to get comfortable with debt, keeping in mind that big debt for property portfolios accumulates over years.

- Negative gearing can be a great tool as long as the property is increasing in value above what you are losing; and properties naturally move from being negatively to positively geared over time.

- Self-managed super funds (SMSFs) can borrow to invest in property, making negative gearing a possibility in this space.

- There are lots of complex rules in buying property through SMSFs, and steep consequences for failure to comply; expert advice is essential if you pursue this path.

- The real reason for investing in property in an SMSF is the end game, when the fund becomes a pension fund, which operates in a zero-tax environment.

- The benefits of investing in super can be considerable, with tax rates much more favourable, but the downside of investing in super is access: you can't get money out of super until you hit a *condition of release*.

- As SMSF property loans are limited recourse, banks will not lend as much of the purchase price of properties, and will usually charge higher interest rates.

- Gearing property in an SMSF allows you to control a much larger asset.

- The negative gearing associated with super property investments has a lesser value, but this is compensated for by the fact that the super won't pay any tax in pension phase.

- Professional help is essential when using SMSFs to invest in property.

7

Structuring your loans

Summer holidays and jigsaw puzzles went hand in hand for me as a kid. They were an ever-present part of my holidays during my youth at my grandparents' holiday house. There was always a puzzle to work on somewhere on a table.

More so than other investments, property is like a really big jigsaw. It might be just one property, but the entire purchasing process can take an incredible amount of time to pull together.

So many different pieces need to fall into place for a property to end up in your possession. At a minimum, you need to traipse through dozens of properties searching for 'the one'. At various stages, the buying process can go weeks with little happening. Then other people will chip in and help things along a little. You'll spend countless hours organising your finances, perhaps fail at auctions a few times, waste hours dealing with agents and lawyers. (And if this is for your home, you'll lose days packing, moving and unpacking.)

It doesn't just happen all at once. But right near the end, the pieces come together very quickly.

This chapter is about a very important piece of the property puzzle — structure. Sounds boring? Don't let that fool you. Structure is a crucial part of this whole property purchasing process. You can't just skip it and move on.

That attitude could, literally, cost you a fortune.

A poor structure can really bugger things up. When I talk about structure, I'm predominantly talking about two things—who owns the property and how the property is financed. The simplest errors, lack of thought, or 'convenient' decision could cost you tens of thousands of dollars. That would almost defeat the purpose of making the investment in the first place.

Think I'm talking rubbish? Well, let me give you simple, but all too common, examples of costly structural mistakes.

The married couple that bought an investment property in joint names, when they were trying to start a family. One partner subsequently spent most of the next five to ten years either unemployed or in part-time employment, while having and raising their kids, while the other partner was consistently earning a salary of more than $100 000 a year.

Cost? Oh, probably tens of thousands of dollars... and counting. This was largely in missed tax deductions because the negative gearing was being claimed jointly against their incomes. Getting a tax deduction on a $0 income is worth, um, nothing. Every year until the property becomes positively geared is going to be expensive for them.

Or another couple who sold their home and wanted to park some cash for about nine months while they built their new residence. Unfortunately, they put the money in the redraw account of an investment property (not an offset account). They could no longer claim a tax deduction on the full loan, but only on the interest on approximately $30 000. It changed the financial viability of the property so much that they had to sell, incurring sales costs, and rebuy another investment property, incurring stamp duty.

Total cost: Around $25 000 in sale costs and stamp duties, not including the capital gains tax bill.

Or the three mates that bought a property together in partnership, who then struggled for years to exit the property at a profit and hold the friendship together. The structure of their loan had an impact on other financial decisions they wanted to make as individuals. (The bigger disaster would have been a destroyed friendship, but they managed to hold that together and come out with a small profit.)

It can get a whole lot worse than that. But it doesn't need to.

By making sure you have the right structures (ownership and loan) in place from the start, you can remove some (but not all) big risks that could otherwise derail or destroy your investment.

Make these decisions before you start looking and certainly before you get your loan (or pre-approval). While no amount of structuring can prepare perfectly for everything that might happen, there are certainly some situations that you should aim to avoid from the outset.

Stopping problems before they occur? Priceless.

Warning: No substitute for legal advice

The advice in this chapter is no substitute for getting proper legal advice. Everyone's situation is different and this book can only cover the basics of legal ownership options and does not take into account your personal situation.

Ownership—who's on the title?

Who's going to own it? If the 'you' is a couple, the ownership options are: one person, the other person, or the couple jointly. Outside of individuals, other property owners can include partnerships, companies, trusts and self-managed super funds (SMSFs). Each is a different legal entity, which comes with differing asset bases, prospects and levels of protection.

If this property thing works out well for you, you'd want to protect the wealth it has created for you, wouldn't you?

The answer is an obvious yes. So, let's shine a light on the ways property can be owned and also, more importantly, how it shouldn't be owned, if asset protection is important to you. And in the second half of this chapter, I'll give you the crucially important section on structuring your loans to maximise your property interests.

Individuals

It seems so obvious, doesn't it? If it's just you, then you might not think you have an option except to buy it in your name. (You do, but I'll come back to that.)

If you're part of a couple, then there are three options: you, me and us.

Buying a property in individual names is the simplest way of doing it. There are no set-up costs and the documents required for borrowing are straightforward. For most individuals, this is the favoured and most cost-effective option.

But from an asset protection perspective, it leaves you (as an individual or a couple) the most vulnerable.

Why wouldn't you own it? There are many reasons, some of which many people don't think of until after it's too late. But the person who holds the property should usually be the person who is least likely to lose it.

'Huh? What the ...?'

Let me explain.

Many occupations run a higher-than-average chance of being sued for mistakes or errors (or plain bad luck) in their line of duty. These occupations include doctors, lawyers and accountants, but can include anyone who works with clients where personal or financial damage can be done. That means almost anyone running a small business. Truck drivers can have accidents, builders can make disastrous errors, restaurant kitchens could poison their customers ... and the damages could run into the hundreds of thousands, even millions.

If one member of a couple is in the category that might get professionally sued, then would you want to protect the property from being lost if that could be avoided?

Let's take Mick and Jane. Jane is an obstetrician and Mick is employed at a bank. They bought the house in joint names. One of Jane's clients sues her over an error and wins millions. As an asset that Jane partly owns, the house must be sold to help pay the damages (she's later declared bankrupt).

However, had the property been bought in Mick's name only, it wouldn't be an asset that could be forced to be sold in this situation.

Similarly, small businesses can go broke. Too many do. If one member of a couple is running a small business—no matter how good they are at it—consideration should be given to having property assets in the name of the other partner (particularly if they are an employee in a low-risk industry). If you're both in positions that could be sued, then stronger consideration should be given to the likes of a family trust.

Divorce and separation—it's all the one pot of money

Some people will have a fear of putting everything in the name of one spouse. What happens if the couple separates?

Family courts nowadays see the whole picture and almost all assets are seen as divisible (including superannuation).

That means that if all $1 million worth of assets (including property, superannuation and other assets) are, for instance, bought in the wife's name, then when it comes to a settlement, the whole $1 million is there to be divided between the parties. Though that doesn't mean it's going to end up being split evenly!

However, if Peter and Minh decide to put all assets in Minh's name and Peter dies, you will also need specialist legal advice in regards to wills.

If you can foresee potential problems in regards to ownership of a property, make an appointment to sit down with a solicitor to discuss the risks and how they might be minimised. You will never be able to negate all risks, but a few hundred dollars could be well spent in minimising potential problems.

Buying with family and friends

With rising property prices, Australians are increasingly looking to co-invest with family and friends. Parents often want to help their kids get into property and offer to buy it with them. Friends who individually don't believe they could afford a property wish to join forces to get a foothold.

As a concept, joining forces and finances to buy property should certainly make it easier, shouldn't it? You can have your cake and …

Actually, hold that cake and don't eat it for a second. You might want it to throw at someone.

Me.

Yup, I'm about to make myself really unpopular to many of you. I've got plenty of tips and warnings in this book. And this is going to be one of the strongest. If you're considering buying property with others... DON'T DO IT!

Avoid going into property ownership with others, wherever possible. Property ownership is a complex and risky financial investment at the best of times. Adding another party will, often, double the potential risks involved, by adding big new dimensions to what could go wrong.

While done with the best of intentions, adding extra parties to the deal will dramatically reduce the chances that you'll be able to make a success of your property investment.

Why? Because you lose control in the following ways:

- You won't necessarily get to determine when you can sell the property. You may wish to hold it, but they want to sell it. Somebody has lost their job, is feeling under financial pressure, or just wants out. There's a divorce, a family bust-up, or just a general sense of panic.

- One party may wish to improve the property, while the other doesn't want to spend any money (or can't afford it at that time).

- One party thinks a particular real estate agent is doing a terrible job, but your partners disagree. You want to sack the agent, but you don't have the power.

They're the main, but by no means the only, potential problems.

Let me put it this way: You are tipping *hundreds of thousands of dollars of your money* into this investment — money that is either your own or that you're responsible for repaying to a bank.

Do you really want to have to seek agreement, or potentially negotiate, with someone else on whether you can or can't do something to protect this *massive* investment that you've made?

I've seen it turn ugly on too many occasions. Too much money gets blown on lawyers. Friends now won't speak to each other. Family functions get boycotted.

By no means are things guaranteed to get ugly. Far from it. But the risk of friction between owners when there is only one owner is zero. With multiple owners, it rises exponentially.

If you can avoid buying with others, do. This might mean buying a smaller place on your own, or something a little further out, or waiting until you've saved a bigger deposit, or until your income has increased.

If you can't afford to buy a property on your own, then should you really be buying a property?

However, if you intend to ignore that advice, and I know many will, then I wish you the best of luck and smooth sailing with your property partners.

There are ways of making it work. One way of taking out bickering about management issues is for one investor, preferably one with the most property-investment experience, to take majority ownership of the property, under a *tenants-in-common* ownership structure (more on this later in this chapter). This involves other investors taking minority shareholdings and effectively coming along for the ride on the investment. This still has its dangers, but at least management control will be understood from the start. Again, seek legal advice on the structure, because it has ramifications you need to understand.

Parental assistance — kicking them out the door

It's natural for parents to want to give their kids a leg up into their first property. That might just be because parents are sick of their kids hanging around the family home and they're willing to take their chances with empty nest syndrome to get their home back.

For many, it will be a simple gift for part of the deposit — perhaps a few thousand dollars, perhaps tens of thousands of dollars.

If it's going to be more than just a pure cash gift, it can get quite complicated, and financial and legal advice will be required. There are a number of options, including becoming a security/equity guarantor on a loan or becoming a servicing guarantor (offering part of your income to service the loan), the latter of which has become very difficult for banks to offer with changes in the law.

Security guarantors typically put up some of their own home as security for their child's loan. While this is fairly popular, it is often done without a full understanding of the dangers it poses. People can lose their own home if their children fail to meet the repayments on their home.

(continued)

137

Parental assistance — kicking them out the door *(cont'd)*

Depending on how far parents are willing to go, their home's equity could be used to save the kids from having to pay lender's mortgage insurance, or it could be used to assist the kids to borrow more than they would otherwise have been able to.

But there are many things that can go wrong — and one way of looking at this is that if the kids haven't done the hard yards to save what they needed to save, are they really ready to take on home ownership? That's a decision for parents to make. If parents want to help their kids, there are lenders out there who will allow them to do so.

Parents be warned: If you put your home up as equity, banks WILL sell your home, if necessary, to make sure their loan is repaid.

If you do wish to proceed with a multi-person investment, here is a list to help reduce the risks involved.

1   Make sure you have a proper written agreement covering who will be in charge of ongoing management decisions, how decisions will be made, when money will be spent.

2   Have an exit strategy. Is there a generally agreed holding period? It should be in writing and with an indication, if not a hard date, of when the property will be sold.

3   Cover what would occur if one person wants to sell, but another party doesn't. Can one buy the other out? How would a price be agreed?

4   Determine the *sinking* fund to cover longer-term maintenance issues. How big does the buffer need to be and under what circumstances will the partners be obligated to tip money into it?

5   Determine the emergency fund — how much and when would it be required from partners?

6   Decide who is in charge of hiring and firing the agent and deciding on tenants.

7   Decide how insurance issues will be handled.

8   Decide how stalemates will be decided, or who will be consulted to settle any disputes (an external party you would trust to make an informed independent decision).

That is a start for discussions around a legal agreement that you should have before entering into any sort of shared arrangement. You should see a lawyer in regards to drawing up a property agreement.

Multiple buyers: Some banks are friendlier than others

What many people who enter into a purchase with other buyers don't realise is the impact it will have on their future ability to borrow.

Most banks assume the worst from the point of view of being able to service the loan. That is, if you are one of three owners, they will assume that you will have to repay the entire debt yourself, but with only one-third of the income. Jointly, you have loans for $450 000, of which $150 000 is notionally yours. Imagine the impact on your ability to get a loan, if you had to service the whole $450 000. Well, that's what most lenders assume.

Some banks offer lending products that are more understanding and flexible than others in regards to this strategy. Contact a reputable mortgage broker if you are considering buying with multiple owners.

Joint tenancy

Joint tenancy is where there is more than one owner and each owner shares an equal portion of the property; and the *right of survivorship* means that in the event of the death of one of the owners, the remaining owners receive the ownership of the deceased's property evenly.

If there are three owners of the property and one dies, the remaining two owners move from owning one-third each to one-half each.

This is the way that most couples own their home, if they own it jointly. When one partner dies, the living spouse inherits the entire property.

From a property investment perspective, joint tenancy works best for two individuals, or a couple, who have similar incomes (or are in the same marginal tax bracket) and are likely to remain that way.

Tenants-in-common

The other option for individuals to hold property is known as *tenants-in-common* (or TIC). Tenants-in-common are not required to hold equal portions (though they can) and, as a main distinction, can leave their ownership of the property in their wills to whoever they wish.

For example, you could have three owners, with one having 60 per cent of the ownership and the other two having 20 per cent of the ownership, or any mix, for any number of potential investors. In the example where there is a clear majority owner (greater than 50 per cent), the minority investors might be willing to accept that they have less, or no, say in the running of the property. Any shareholder agreement that they signed should probably reflect that the majority shareholder has management control of the property and the two minority shareholders, while able to voice their opinion on matters, are effectively coming along for the investment ride.

Where friends or family wish to purchase a property together, then using a tenants-in-common structure, where one person has majority control (even if it's 51–49 per cent) can reduce the potential for arguments over the management of the property.

A TIC owner can also sell their portion when they wish (though other buyers would likely be limited as they would have to deal with existing partners). This would usually mean potential purchasers are limited to one of the other TIC partners. That the ownership of the property can also be dealt with in the deceased's will can also mean that the other partners end up with a new partner they had not bargained on when they purchased the property.

TIC is often used by couples to hold property as 99 per cent in the higher-earning spouse's name and 1 per cent in the lower-earning spouse's name, then leaving the remainder to the other surviving spouse in the will. This allows the majority of the property to be tax-deductible for the higher-earning spouse.

Self-managed super funds (SMSFs)

It often seems like property ownership by SMSFs is the new kid on the block. It's not—SMSFs have always been able to own investment property. What is new is that SMSFs, since 2007, have been able to *borrow* to buy property. This has dramatically opened up the number of SMSFs that can buy property.

It is a highly complex way of holding investment property (if it is geared) and I discuss this in chapter 6. Anyone considering buying geared property in an SMSF is strongly advised to seek advice from a well-qualified financial adviser and/or SMSF-specialist lawyer.

Other significant property holding structures

While individuals and SMSFs are currently among the most popular ways to hold property, they are not the only ways. Other methods include trusts (discretionary, fixed and unit trusts), companies and partnerships. While each of these structures has some great qualities for property investors, specialist legal and financial advice before entering into these ownership structures is recommended.

1 *Trusts.* Legal entities where trustees hold assets on behalf of beneficiaries, under the terms of a trust deed. Trusts can be complex legal entities and one of their main uses is for asset protection.

2 *Partnerships.* Where two or more investors get together, usually for larger projects, to pool their capital and talent to buy, manage and (usually) sell property. A downside of partnerships can be, in some cases, unlimited liability for the partners and difficulty in exiting the partnership without it coming to a natural conclusion on sale of the property.

3 *Companies.* Shareholders are the ultimate owners of companies and shareholders' liability is usually limited to the value of their shares. While companies can own property, they are usually the most expensive holding vehicle, because of regulatory requirements, which will usually require professionals to assist with set-up and ongoing management.

Structuring debt

The next part of the puzzle is how you best structure this monstrous—at minimum it's huge, but will be monstrous if you're building a portfolio—debt that will come with the property you're purchasing.

For some, the answer is simple. If you're buying your first property (home or investment) with a healthy deposit, the answers are generally going to be reasonably straightforward. That doesn't mean you can just slap this thing together, or that you should necessarily just take a bank's recommendation. (I assure you, they will have their own best interests at heart, not yours. Mortgage brokers at least have a degree of independence.)

And anyone who has aspirations of building a property portfolio needs to get things right from the start. Sometimes when you get things wrong, it simply can't be undone. Other times, it can be undone, but it can be very expensive (in money and/or time).

There is no perfect set-up that can be laid out in a book like this. That's because we're all different. There are many base scenarios, which I lay out in this chapter and elsewhere in this book, but you will inevitably need to tailor those solutions to your circumstances. If you can confidently put together the basics for yourself, great. If not, get a mortgage broker involved.

Your first home loan

As discussed in chapter 6, the best way to buy your first home is with a big deposit. Having a deposit of 20 to 25 per cent—depending on first-home buyer concessions and grants in your state—will mean that you won't have to pay lender's mortgage insurance (LMI—see later in this chapter).

If you borrow above 80 per cent, you'll likely have to pay LMI.

In figure 7.1, I show how best to set up your loans for a reasonably straightforward home loan.

Figure 7.1: setting up your offset account

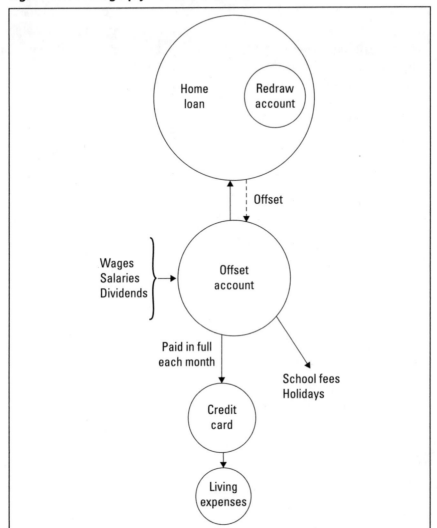

In most cases, you will simply want one loan (with a redraw option), one offset account, possibly one credit card, and away you go (see table 4.3 on p. 60). If you want to have all of your loan as variable-rate (see chapter 4), have all of your income put in the one offset account and pay your mortgages from there. This set-up will be efficient, making the most of your offset account and potentially benefiting also from the credit card.

However, if you want to split your loan to have it part fixed and part variable, then you will end up with two loans. This will usually still come with one offset account, which will save you interest on the variable loan only (though banking products are evolving quickly). As displayed in figure 7.2, it will usually be most efficient (as in, save you the most money) to have all loans paid from the same offset account.

Figure 7.2: setting up your offset account for multiple loans

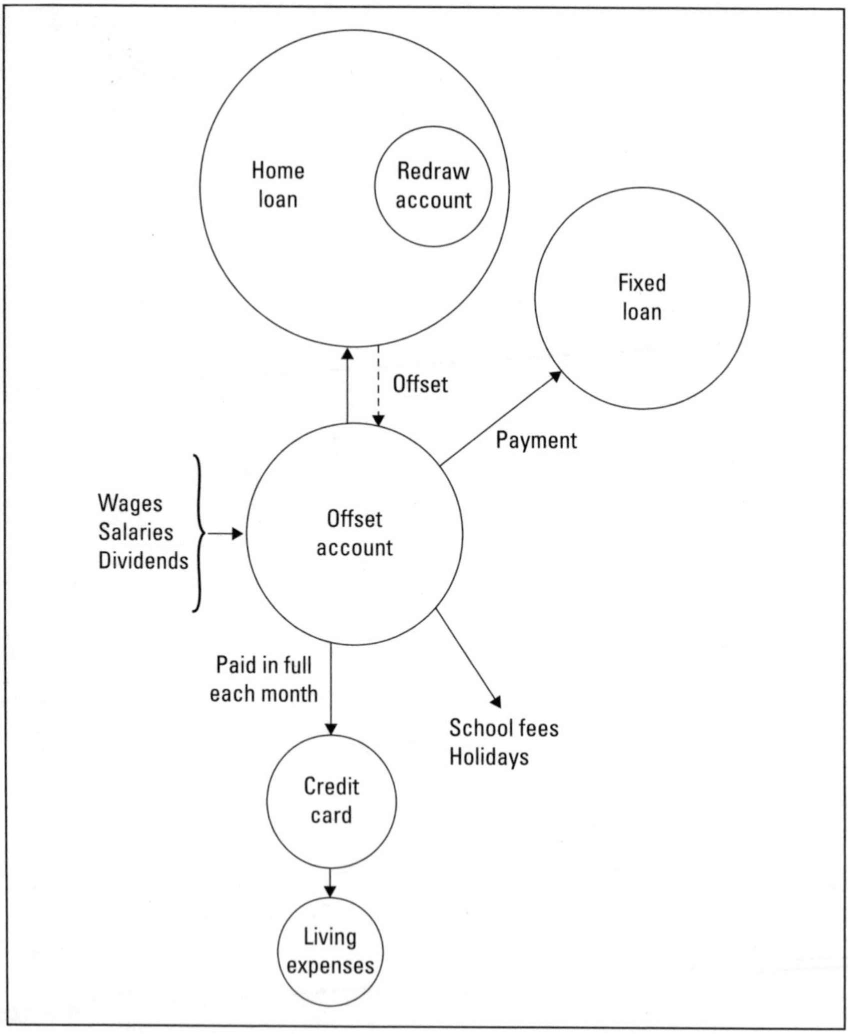

Technically, you can have any number of loans against the one property, though some banks will limit you to two, or will charge extra fees for extra splits. Having extra loans can be useful for a car loan, an investment loan, or line of credit, and many banks can accommodate this.

What if there's a chance I might turn my home into an investment?

If this is a possibility at some stage, then getting the structure right at the start is crucial to how successful the property will be as an investment, as well as how low the mortgage is on your next home. This could save you thousands of dollars, potentially each year after you turn it into an investment property.

I lay this out in detail in chapter 5. Essentially, if your home is going to be turned into an investment property, don't pay down the loan. Keep as much of your own money for the deposit on the next home. At the same time, you wish to keep the debt on the current home as high as possible to keep the maximum deductions you can claim when it becomes an investment property.

You should consider the following:

- Make sure you use an offset account, not a redraw account. They both save you the same interest. However, the tax office sees redraw accounts very differently. This could affect your tax deductions when you convert this into an investment property (see chapter 5).

- Have an interest-only loan for your main home loan. Put any extra savings that you haven't paid off the principal into your offset account and allow that balance to build. (Though the temptation to spend might be greater, which you will need to weigh up.)

- Consider using a lender that allows you to have multiple offset accounts, so that you can still park your longer-term savings in a separate account from your normal savings.

- Keep receipts for all major improvements to the house. They might become tax-deductible when you rent the house out.

The distinction between *offset* and *redraw* is particularly important from a tax perspective.

This sort of structure will allow you to take all of your savings to your new home when you move into it. For example, say you buy a home for $500 000 with a $450 000 loan, using the structure I've outlined here. Over the next five years, you manage to save $90 000 in your offset account, so you're only paying interest on this loan for $360 000 ($450 000 minus $90 000).

Then you buy another home. By using the offset account correctly, you can take the $90 000 as a deposit or equity for the new home. And when you convert it to an investment property, you will get a tax deduction on the interest for the full $450 000 again.

(If you had used a redraw account, the ATO would allow a tax deduction on the interest of $360 000.)

If you eventually decide not to rent it out, but to sell it (to take the equity with you to your new property), the above structure will mean that you won't be in a worse position—no damage will have been done, *if you have been able to save the money and not spend it.* And at any time, you can switch to principal and interest, or make extra repayments into your redraw account.

Your first investment property

The structure of the loan for your first investment property will depend on a few things. Do you already have a home loan? If not, are you intending to buy a home in the future? If owning a home to live in is not part of your plans, then is this likely to be your only investment property, or are you looking to build a portfolio?

Already have a home

If you already have a home loan, your aim should be to have a structure that allows you to maximise the tax deductions on your investment property, while minimising the amount of interest you pay on your home loan (which is not a tax deduction).

Some people see this and believe that it must be trickery—how can you pay less on your home loan? It's this simple. If you had an extra $10 000, would you use it to pay down your home loan, or your investment property loan?

Your home loan, of course.

So, then, it's just a matter of creating that extra $10 000 (or $1000, or $5000 or $20 000—the amount doesn't matter). How do you do that?

Take an investment property loan of $400 000, on 6.5 per cent over 30 years. If the loan is principal and interest, the repayments would be $2528 a month. If it is interest-only, the monthly repayment would be $2167. The difference is $361 a month, or $4332 a year.

The owners of this investment property also have a home loan of $450 000, on which the monthly repayments are $2844. By diverting the extra $361 a month into paying down their home loan, they will shave nearly eight years (seven years and 11 months) off their home loan and save approximately $176 000 in interest.

They will also benefit in other ways. They will maintain higher tax deductions on their investment property, which could also be directed to paying down the home loan faster.

It's powerful stuff.

Figure 7.3 (overleaf) differs from the previous figures in that there is rent coming in to the offset and an investment mortgage to pay also.

Figure 7.3: setting up your offset account for a property portfolio

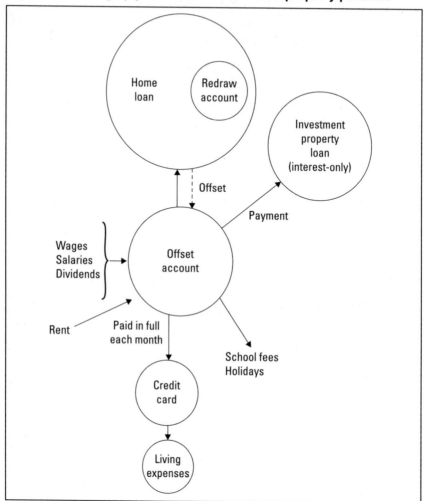

So, in order to take advantage of these potential benefits, you are looking to use this model to set up your loans in roughly the following way:

- on your investment property, you pay interest-only

- on your home loan, you pay principal and interest

- have all incoming money paid into your offset account, including rent from the investment property

- set up direct debits from your offset account for bills, including the credit card, to be paid on their due dates.

Looking to buy a home after investment property

This is the situation I found myself in. I told Mrs DebtMan (then my girlfriend) that I wanted to buy a home. She said: 'No, you can't buy a home until *we* can buy a home.' She was not long out of uni, had no savings and some credit card debt.

But I desperately wanted to buy. I gave her one year to save for a home, but I decided I would buy an investment property in the meantime. And off I went.

I had two choices. I could use all of my then savings to keep the loan on the investment as low as possible. Or, I could get a larger loan and hold on to some of my savings, so that I could put it towards buying our home (which happened about 15 months later).

The second option will often work better, although consideration always needs to be given to the fact that if you buy an investment property first, you will not get the benefits of first-home owner grants, or first-home buyer stamp duty concessions (see chapter 5 for a bigger discussion). Here's why.

Let's say a couple has $110 000 in savings. For whatever their personal reason, they want to buy an investment property first, then a home in a year or three.

The investment property is worth $450 000. They could use their entire deposit to effectively pay the 20 per cent deposit (to escape lender's mortgage insurance) and stamp duty, leaving them with a loan on the investment property of approximately $360 000.

Or they could pay for 10 per cent ($45 000), plus stamp duty and costs (say $20 000), which would use approximately $65 000 of their savings, leaving $45 000 in savings for when they buy their own place. They should pay interest-only on the debt of their investment property and save what they would have had to pay in principal payments towards their deposit for the new home they will eventually purchase.

And they can start to build their savings again.

Other advantages and disadvantages:

- Advantage: They have maintained a higher tax-deductibility on the investment loan.

- Advantage: The eventual loan for their home, which is non-deductible, will be lower as a result.

- Disadvantage: They will have to pay some LMI for borrowing more than 80 per cent of the value of the investment property.

Investment only

You're not looking to buy a home. You're happy to rent forever (or for the foreseeable future anyway) and want to buy an investment property, or potentially build your investment portfolio.

Years ago, banks wanted you to be paying principal on at least one of your loans, but now they are usually happy for you to pay interest-only on your investment loans. If your bank isn't, another one will be.

If you just want to buy one investment property and won't be buying a home, then your choices are to either pay interest-only and use your money to build investments elsewhere (or enjoy a nicer lifestyle), or pay principal and interest to help build your equity faster.

It can still be a good idea to pay interest-only and use an offset account for your savings, which will minimise the interest you have to pay each month.

Building a property portfolio

And if you're looking to build a property portfolio... getting the structure right early is particularly important.

Building a valuable property portfolio is usually a decades-long process. It starts with a single property, for which the rules I've just outlined generally apply. If you have a home, use the offset account to keep interest payments on that debt to a minimum.

If you don't own a home, but intend to in the future, it is crucial that you use an offset account, and not a redraw account (as explained in chapter 5).

When the 'best' isn't right for you

The way that you deal with money is like a fingerprint. It's unique. And what might be the 'best' way of minimising interest payments and maximising deductions might not be what works with your money DNA.

Some people will want separate savings/offset accounts for separate loans, with rent going into related accounts and payments for individual properties coming from those separate accounts. If that is going to allow you to understand your financial position and track payments properly, then you should do that.

Or, perhaps, having one account for the home loan and a second account that deals with transactions for one or many properties would be best for you.

The advice in this book is designed to get you to understand the most efficient methods—from a tax and savings perspective—but that doesn't always work for individuals. Just be aware that some choices might cost you a little more.

But see the next section for how you can potentially get the best of both worlds.

Multiple offset accounts—the new star on Mortgage Street

In recent times, banks have started offering packages with multiple offset accounts to assist you with managing your own money, which work together to reduce interest on your loans.

For example, you might have, say, three offset accounts for your home loan of $530 000. The first account might have $15 000 in it, the second has $5000 and the third has $8000. For that month, you will only pay interest on $502 000 ($530 000 minus $28 000).

This is a great innovation in banking and allows for many different types of money personalities, particularly couples, to benefit from offset accounts.

Yours, mine and ours

From my experience as a financial adviser and mortgage broker, I understand that it's actually the norm for couples to have separate money. They will often have an account for each partner and then potentially a joint account. The joint account is the account from which shared bills are paid and they often both pay a weekly or monthly amount into that account for that purpose. But they still have their own money in their own accounts for their own spending.

Unfortunately, if there is only one offset, but three accounts are required, then there is always going to be money that is in regular savings accounts, earning interest on which tax has to be paid.

Being able to have multiple offset accounts attached to the one home loan means a couple can have separate money, if that's what works best for them, but still have every dollar saving them interest on their home loan.

Separate accounts

Multiple offset accounts can also work well for people who like to have money separated into different accounts for different purposes. These could be for any reason, including for travel, medical costs, emergency funds, to buy cars, to pay bills and so on.

Obviously, multiple offset accounts are often perfect for organising your finances like this (though some of the providers have rules about how much money must be deposited in each account each month to avoid fees). But having two or three offset accounts can be useful for, particularly, having separate accounts for general banking, and short-term and long-term savings.

Having multiple banking partners

There are often good reasons for having all of your banking with one lender. Often, for an annual fee of $200 to $400, you can get very good value from a banking package, including loan discounts, free banking, free credit cards, and so on (see the section on professional packages in chapter 4).

However, there will be times when you both *want* to deal with multiple banks and *need* to deal with multiple banks.

This could be because your existing bank won't lend to you at the time that you need the money, or they won't lend for the particular property you want to buy, or any one of a number of different reasons. Sometimes, the bank you wish to deal with will come back with a valuation that doesn't suit, or make possible, what you want to do.

Some of my clients have wanted to grow their property portfolios fairly aggressively. And, at some points, their preferred lender has let them down. Often, you will need to use another bank who will play ball on terms that are acceptable to you.

You might develop a good relationship with a particular bank. But don't swallow everything they say hook, line and sinker. Banks do take their clients for granted—don't expect them to ever volunteer to reduce the interest rate you're paying, unless you threaten to leave or complain occasionally—and sometimes they need to show some love to you, or you should threaten to go elsewhere.

Structuring of multiple loans

For those who are buying a second property—whether that second property is going to be a home or an investment property—some thought needs to be put into the structure of the loans.

As you're building an asset base of properties and associated debt, important questions need to be answered along the way, including whether your relationship will be with one bank or many.

But before we go on, there is something important that you need to understand, regarding the ways that security can be taken by a bank to cover their loans.

Cross-collateralisation

Cross-collateralisation means that a bank holds security over more than one property for a loan. Most commonly, a borrower might have, for example, two properties and there are two loans on the properties. The securities on the two properties are *crossed*, which means that the bank can sell both properties, if it needs to, to settle the loans.

This can be a particular problem when a borrower deals directly with a bank. Banks seem to have as a default setting that they suggest cross-collateralisation to clients. And you can understand why—they have security over more properties and that gives them greater assurance that they can get their money back if trouble with the borrower is afoot.

If it can possibly be avoided, it should be. If you have multiple properties and growing equity in those properties, then it can usually be done. And, if you have sufficient equity, you can often just insist that the properties not be cross-collateralised. Figure 7.4 shows how loans and properties can be interconnected via cross-collateralisation.

Figure 7.4: an example of cross-collateralisation

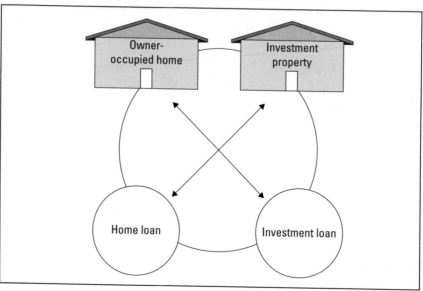

Stand-alone loans

How can cross-collateralisation be avoided when you're borrowing more than 100 per cent of the property (to take in stamp duty) and if you want to avoid LMI? Potentially by structuring it as two loans against separate properties.

Say your home is worth $800 000 and there is a home loan of $250 000 on that. You wish to purchase an investment property for $500 000, with total debt for that purchase of $530 000.

This property loan can be structured by having three loans over the two properties. There's the existing home loan, then a loan for 80 per cent of the value of the investment property against that property (loan of $400 000), with the remaining $130 000 against the home. The final $130 000 will still be tax-deductible debt, because the *purpose of the loan* is for the investment property. In table 7.1 I show how this loan can be structured without having to incur lender's mortgage insurance, despite technically borrowing more than 100 per cent of the value of the investment property.

Table 7.1: stand-alone loans

	Value	Loan	Loan-to-valuation ratio (LVR)
Home	$800 000	$250 000	31.25%
Home		$130 000	16.25%
Investment property	$500 000	$400 000	80.00%
Total	$1 300 000	$780 000	60.00%

In this example, the total loan to valuation (LVR) over all of the properties is only 60 per cent. There is no LMI to pay, because the combined debt on each property is below 80 per cent.

Investors: Ensure debt facilities are ready to roll

When it comes to buying an investment property, it is important to note that, if you are going to completely fund the property purchase with debt, it needs to be done that way from the beginning.

That is, you cannot pay for, say, the 10 per cent deposit with your own savings, then repay yourself when the loans settle. You should have

(continued)

> **Investors: Ensure debt facilities are ready to roll *(cont'd)***
>
> finance in place before signing a contract to be able to pay that initial 5 or 10 per cent deposit with debt.
>
> There are many ways of doing this, but it's best to speak to a mortgage broker before looking for a property to purchase, to make sure that it will suit your circumstances.
>
> For example, as in table 7.1, if you did organise for a facility against your existing home to cover the 20 per cent plus stamp duties of your investment property, then you would use this facility to pay the initial deposit on your property. Then, at settlement, the bank would put 80 per cent against the investment property (making 90 per cent so far), and the remaining 10 per cent plus stamp duties on the loan against the home.
>
> Why is this important? For tax deductibility. If you pay the initial deposit with savings, you won't get a tax deduction on the debt used to repay your savings. So making sure that it is funded by debt from day one is critical, or this could be an expensive error.

Lender's mortgage insurance (LMI)

LMI has been raised many times throughout this book. It's a nasty, often large, charge that is essentially the bank getting you to pay the premium for an insurance policy for them. This is in case you fail on your loan and the bank has to sell your property, but the property isn't worth enough to repay the loan.

The reason LMI is needed is probably best explained with an example. Let's say Ajit and Susan bought a home for $500 000 and borrowed $450 000 (90 per cent of the value of the property).

A year after they bought the property, the economy turns south. As the result of the downturn, Ajit loses his job and they can't afford to continue paying the mortgage. The bank moves in to sell the property to recover the loan. However, the downturn has affected property prices and the property only fetches $410 000—not enough to repay the $450 000 borrowed.

Lender's mortgage insurance then allows the bank to make a claim with the mortgage insurer against the loss of that $40 000 and other costs.

As a result, anyone who borrows more than 80 per cent of the value of a property is generally liable to pay LMI. This charge will be passed on directly by the bank to the borrower.

The rate at which LMI is charged is exponential and can also jump far higher when the value of the property being purchased increases. In table 7.2, we use the $500 000 purchase price from our previous example.

Table 7.2: lender's mortgage insurance (LMI) premiums

Loan-to-valuation ratio (LVR)	Loan amount	LMI premium	LMI premium as % of loan
80%	$400 000	$0	0%
81%	$405 000	$2405	0.594%
82%	$410 000	$2435	0.594%
83%	$415 000	$2592	0.625%
84%	$420 000	$3700	0.881%
85%	$425 000	$4006	0.943%
86%	$430 000	$4716	1.097%
87%	$435 000	$4813	1.106%
88%	$440 000	$6132	1.394%
89%	$445 000	$6706	1.507%
90%	$450 000	$8533	1.897%
91%	$455 000	$12 917	2.839%
92%	$460 000	$13 343	2.901%
93%	$465 000	$15 252	3.280%
94%	$470 000	$15 416	3.280%
95%	$475 000	$17 242	3.630%

Note: For consistency, we have used the same major lender in the above calculations, with a house purchased in Victoria. Other banks may use insurers whose charges and percentages might differ from those above. LMI-charge percentages may increase for higher-priced properties.

As you can see, it increases relatively smoothly... until the loan goes above a 90 per cent LVR. Above 90 per cent, LMI spikes, as insurers and banks charge for the increased risk of loan failure. Understand that this is an insurance premium that *does not cover you*. The bank is passing on the cost of the insurance premium it has to pay to cover *itself* against your potential failure to repay the loan.

Obviously, if you're going to borrow more money, your repayments are going to be higher also. But LMI is the really significant difference between buying your first home sooner rather than later. Most of the rest of the costs of purchase do not change depending on the amount borrowed.

If you have the patience to save 20 per cent plus legals, then that is a great target to achieve and all power to you. For most, having enough to ensure your loan is below 90 per cent of the property's purchase price (and therefore with a reduced LMI premium) will be sufficient and will allow people to purchase their homes sooner.

LMI: Advantages for buyers

LMI means that buyers can purchase properties sooner than they might otherwise be able to. If LMI didn't exist, banks would probably insist on minimum deposits of 20 per cent plus stamp duty and costs.

With many lenders, the actual LMI premium can be *capitalised*—that is, it can be added to the loan. In our previous example, the $450 000 loan would become a loan of $458 533.

For investors, if the LMI premium is added to the loan, the interest on that premium therefore becomes a tax deduction (a small benefit that will add up over the years).

Another reason for paying LMI could be in keeping some of your money for yourself, as raised earlier in this chapter, potentially to fund your own home purchase.

That is, if you had $130 000 in savings to buy a $500 000 investment property, but you were also wanting to buy a home in a year or so, then you might only use $80 000 of those savings to pay a 10 per cent deposit and cover your stamp duty, leaving you with a loan of approximately $450 000, which would require paying LMI.

But it would allow you to keep $50 000 in savings for your future home. This is something that needs to be weighed up by individual circumstances.

Property purchasing principles

It's not all about the house and the garden! Those attributes for the property are really important, either for you to live in or for you to make money from as an investment property.

But there are plenty of other 1 percenters that you need to get right. And those 1 percenters include making sure you get both the ownership and banking structures right.

These are not matters that you want to get wrong, as the financial consequences can be devastating. They can potentially raise the risk of you losing your property, can cost tens of thousands of dollars to fix and, sometimes, cannot be fixed at all and just become an expensive black hole for cash.

Don't risk it. Don't do this on your own unless you're absolutely certain that you've got it right. You're far better off talking to the required professionals—be they mortgage brokers, financial advisers, accountants or solicitors—to get personalised advice than to risk getting it horribly wrong.

And just to ram it home ... here are the key points to take away from this chapter.

- Failure to properly structure your loans can end up costing you a lot of money—it really pays to take the time to get it right.
- Whose name is on the title, whether you're buying alone, with a partner or family or friends, is an important decision with many potential repercussions.
- If you are going to pursue a multi-person investment property, make sure you have a proper written agreement about the various factors involved in maintaining an investment property.
- Joint tenancy is one way to structure a multi-person investment, but it works best for two individuals with similar incomes. When

one owner in a joint tenancy dies, their share is automatically divided among the remaining partners.

- Tenants-in-common is another option, where not all partners have to have equal portions of the property, and the partners can technically sell at any time or leave ownership of the property to whoever they desire in their will.

- Other ways to hold property include SMSFs, trusts, partnerships and companies.

- The structure of your debt is incredibly important to get right, and whether it's your first home, whether you plan on turning your home into an investment property, or it's your first investment property, different factors will have to be taken into account.

- If you already have a home, are looking to buy your home after your investment property, are only planning on owning investment property, or are planning on building a property portfolio, your situation needs individual consideration.

- Loan products with multiple offset accounts can be great tools for organising your finances.

- Sometimes multiple banking partners will be required over the life of your property investing.

- Multiple loans will be required if you want to invest in multiple properties, which involves more structuring considerations.

- You can secure multiple properties through cross-collateralisation or through stand-alone loans.

- Lender's mortgage insurance is the cost of the insurance premium the bank has to pay to cover itself against your potential failure to repay the loan; it passes that cost on to you.

8

And now for the property purchase

If we were to use a plane analogy, I can tell you where you'd be. You're in the cockpit. The cargo is loaded and you've pushed back from the terminal. You're taxiing to the runway and you're pretty much ready for take-off.

But there are always some last-minute preflight checks required. And failing to do some of them could make you crash. Don't be in any doubt about that. There are so many moving parts with a property purchase.

Property is different to other forms of investment that you can make. When you're buying shares, or deciding on a term deposit, or buying a managed fund, there aren't nearly as *many* things that can go wrong. Property is such a big individual asset, where *you* are the one investing hundreds of thousands of dollars and *you* are the one taking management control.

When you buy this baby, you're stuck with it. A property purchase is not a decision you can change your mind on easily. Once you've signed that contract, it's generally too late—you've got the property and its potential problems. So take the time to make those final checks.

But you *are* taxiing. I'm now assuming you're ready to search for your home or investment, or have even identified your target. You might have pretty much agreed on a price, or have decided what you are willing to pay at auction.

Importantly, hopefully, you haven't signed yet.

Before signing the contract

Whether you are buying via private sale or at auction, you will have to sign a contract. Importantly, the vendor also needs to sign in order for your contract to be accepted.

The rules for contracts vary between states (and the differences are too numerous to go into here). You will need a specialist solicitor or conveyancer on your team for your property purchase, so you are best getting one of them to talk you through what is required, before you sign and *after* they have checked the contract and associated documents for anything that could pop up.

Building and pest inspections

Getting a building and pest inspection can alert you to major problems with your potential property purchase. Would you buy the property if it required restumping, if the electrical wires were nearly shot, if the timber in the house had been infested with termites, or if there were major leakage problems throughout?

These are just a few of the hundreds of potential problems that these inspections might uncover. It's rare that houses don't have problems of some description, even brand new properties.

It's best not to risk it. Get the inspections done. They can be annoying, particularly if you're buying at auction and have missed out a few times, but imagine if you did them three times for auctions that you missed out on, then didn't do it for a fourth and that one turned out to be the one with the big issues.

They will generally cost a few hundred dollars each, perhaps $800 or so for both building and pest inspections, but will alert you to problems that your untrained eye might not see. Some of these problems will be minor and won't affect your decision. Others might make you want to run away.

More importantly, these reports can sometimes be used as bargaining tools during your negotiation process, particularly when you are the only party interested in buying the property. If there is a lot of work to be done, point it out to the agent. It can sometimes be used to talk down the price. Agents won't like it, but they are usually keen to seal the deal and if it's warranted, they will make sure their vendor is realistic about the price they want.

Hire a conveyancer

The act of transferring ownership of a property from one person or entity to another is called *conveyancing*. This process is usually handled by a solicitor or specialist conveyancing firm.

Depending on the property, they will usually charge between $500 and $1500. They will handle the actual transfer of the property purchase after contracts have been signed.

But if you only include them after the sale, then you're missing an important function that they will usually do for you as part of their services. And that is doing a quick check of the contract, before the sale, to find out if there are any hidden nasties.

The most common hidden nasties can include:

- *Overlays.* Particularly heritage and public acquisition (for example, the government being able to compulsorily buy your property to make way for a freeway).

- *Flooding zones.* If your property is in a flooding zone, your bank might not accept the security and insurers might not accept the risk.

- *Vendor's rights.* Make sure the vendor has the right to sell the property.

- *Notices.* Are there any notices on title, such as bankruptcy, family court issues or outstanding land tax?

- *Zoning.* Properties are usually zoned for residential or commercial use and you need to make sure that your intended use is allowed for the property.

- *Special conditions.* Sometimes there are some that might not be acceptable.

Some special conditions might be acceptable in a contract, such as penalty interest to be paid by the purchaser if settlement is delayed because of problems at their end (such as financing). But vendor's solicitors have been known to put unreasonable conditions into contracts that might need to be challenged before a contract is signed, such as the purchaser having to pay the vendor's bridging finance costs, accommodation charges and removalist costs.

Specialist solicitors know what words they are looking for when they look at the pre-contract and contract documents, so can usually find this information very quickly and advise you of any hairy conditions that you might want to challenge or potentially walk away from.

Subject to clauses

On some occasions, you may wish to put your own clauses or conditions into a contract. If you're unsure if your finance has been approved, or you wish to agree on a price before ordering a building and pest inspection, then you can often have these clauses inserted into your offer in the agreement/contract.

Your conveyancer can also help walk you through this process.

Also, be aware that you are generally not allowed to put conditions or *subject to* clauses into a contract when you have purchased at auction. You need to have answered all of your questions before you put your hand up to bid, or at least have negotiated those conditions with the vendor and received a favourable response in writing before the auction starts.

Dealing with real estate agents

Now, understand that nothing I am about to say here is to denigrate real estate agents. There are good and bad agents (as all professions have their good and bad eggs).

But dealing with agents can sometimes be frustrating.

In my experience, a lot of the frustration in dealing with real estate agents can be overcome in your own mind by understanding where agents are coming from.

Real estate agents are hired by vendors/sellers to sell their property at the highest price possible. But understand this: *real estate agents usually don't get paid unless the property is sold.*

In practice, this means that real estate agents have a real interest in getting a vendor and a purchaser to *agree on price, whatever that price is.*

Usually, that means they need to talk the buyer up in price and, equally, talk a vendor (their client) down in price. Vendors often have unrealistic expectations of what their property is worth. Agents will usually know this before they take the client on, but will try to condition their client, over time, to understand that they are going to need to accept a lower price if they want their property to sell.

Agents won't get paid unless a contract is signed and the property is sold.

Buyer's advocates

If dealing with real estate agents and entering into negotiations for a property isn't your strong point, or makes you nervous, then consider hiring a buyer's advocate.

Buyer's advocates work for the buyer — with the same potential limitations as to not being paid unless there is a sale. In my experience, however, they are more likely to charge a fee-for-service that means there is less of a conflict. They are also not dealing with one property, but could be dealing with a number of properties for you at once, which also lessens the likelihood of a conflict existing.

If you are considering using a buyer's advocate, meet a few to find out if you believe they will be able to work with you and be able to assist you in purchasing what you would like to purchase. In my opinion, they are probably more useful when purchasing an investment property — they will know what areas are worthwhile looking in and can negotiate without the emotion that experienced real estate agents will smell on you from a mile away.

The good ones can also be very good in assisting with higher-end home purchases too. But as buying a home is more emotional, often it can be better to find the home that you're after and get them to negotiate on price for you.

Auctions versus private sales

Vendors get to choose how they wish to sell their property. And while there are other options, the vast majority of residential properties in Australia are sold via either private sale or auction.

Private sales are more popular in Australia and involve the vendor setting a price for which they will sell the property. This price is usually negotiable. Negotiations on a price and/or conditions can take days or weeks (even months).

As noted earlier in this chapter, you can't put conditions on the sale of a property bought at auction. If you are going to have any conditions, make sure you negotiate those before the auction and get the answers in writing.

Offer accepted!

Negotiating a price with a vendor is equal parts art, acting and science … and definitely an entire book on its own! In any case, it's too technical and detailed for this book to cover. So, for now, I'll assume that you have agreed on a price and you're ready to sign, or have just signed, on the dotted line on the *contract of sale*. (For those who are interested, I have covered the whole negotiation phase of buying in some of my other books, including *Property Investing For Dummies*, Wiley, 2013.)

Congratulations!

However, it's not over yet. There are still a number of very important things that you will need to do to make sure that you end up with this property.

You will have to organise the deposit. Depending on which state you live in, and whether you've negotiated something before the agreement, you will usually need to write a cheque to cover a deposit of 5 or 10 per cent of the purchase price.

If this is your home and you are paying the deposit yourself, the bank will usually help you fund the rest of the property, but might assume you can cover this part yourself. Sign a cheque or organise an EFT transfer to cover the deposit.

For investors, this is actually a very important time to get right and you might need individual advice from your mortgage broker. If you are funding the entire property with debt, you need to make sure that you *pay for this deposit with debt*. See the text box on p. 155 for information on making sure you have this structural issue dealt with at the start. You will need to have the debt facility in place before you sign for the deposit.

Insuring against disaster

The moment that you agree to purchase a property, you have an insurable interest in it. And pardon me, but in order to get this point across, I'm going to use an extreme, though possible, example.

Let's say that you have signed the contract and you have gone home to crack a bottle of bubbly. (You deserve it, so why not?) In 60 days, you'll own this property.

A week later, you get a call from the real estate agent with bad news. The house burned down. Only the fireplace is left standing (which, to quote comedian Jimeoin, 'is a good reminder of where the fire should have been in the first place'). It gets worse: the owner didn't have insurance to cover the house, or the insurance had lapsed, or the place was massively underinsured. It doesn't matter why, but the house isn't covered by insurance.

What happens then?

Well, you're going to panic. There will be contractual disputes. But one thing's for certain: if you're not insured and the seller is not insured, then you're going to be in a horrendous position.

You simply can't trust the other party to do the right thing—you don't know them.

As soon as you buy a property, get some insurance to cover the property. Most major insurers will have lines open on a weekend under which you might be able to organise a cover note. If you have an insurance broker, let them know first thing the following day that you have bought a property and want it covered from day one.

There are other general insurances that you will also need to consider:

- *Contents insurance.* For home buyers, you will need to have your stuff insured when you move in. For landlords, you will need a certain amount of insurance to cover some of the contents that might come with the house, but that aren't covered by building insurance.

- *Landlord's insurance.* This insurance is predominantly to cover you for loss of rent. If your house burns down, landlord's insurance will cover the rental income until the property is rebuilt and rented out again.

- *Common property insurance.* If you are buying in an area with common property between a number of owners, there will need to be insurance to cover public liability. If you are buying into a block, this insurance will normally already be in place (and is actually a legal requirement in most states). But if it isn't, you don't want to be bankrupted by someone hurting themselves on your property—be the one to organise it, but be collaborative with your fellow owners. This insurance usually doesn't cost much and is usually organised by your body corporate or owner's corporation.

Insuring your biggest asset—you

Okay, time to scare the pants off you again. The financial adviser in me is going to take over for a few minutes.

Whether you're buying a home or an investment property, you are doing this often to improve your, or your family's, situation. And you will be doing this by taking on a whopping great debt that is going to take you, and your partner, a decade or two to pay back.

So, what happens if you sign up for a $500 000 mortgage and then die the next day?

You're leaving behind your partner and/or children. Are they going to be able to repay the debt? If you've just bought a home and have a monster mortgage, there's a good chance that the answer will be no.

And what if you got sick or injured and couldn't work for an extended period while you recuperate? Say 6, 12 or 24 months? Would you be able to hold on to your home? The statistics say that the majority of people in this situation would run out of savings and lose the house within a year.

The answer is, again, insurance. This time, it's the life insurances.

There are four main different types of life insurance. They are life insurance, total and permanent disability insurance (TPD), trauma insurance and income protection insurance. And they are all designed to cover different things.

And let's get something straight. While insurance is one of the great grudge purchases ('I know I need this, but I don't really want to pay for it!'), insurance is about making sure that the big, foreseeable risks don't derail your plans, or destroy the lives of your family if you're no longer around.

So, suck it up. This is important. And if you don't love your family enough to at least read this... are you going to tell them, or should I?

Life insurance

Life insurance is simple enough. For whatever reason, you're not breathing anymore. If you've organised insurance, then an insurance payout is made to your super fund, estate or your beneficiaries.

If you were to die, how much money would you want your family to have? Enough to cover all of the debts, including home and/or investment properties? If you have young children, would you want your partner to be able to raise them the way that you had long discussed? This may include private school fees and nanny fees to cover the fact that you or your partner might not be around.

Insurance for large sums for those in their twenties, thirties and forties is usually incredibly cheap.

Structuring your life insurances—get proper advice

More so than any other aspect of financial planning in your life, life insurance can be structured to suit your needs and income. However, the rules are technical and if you're not prepared to do the research to make sure your insurances are done properly, then you need to see a licensed financial adviser.

For example, life and TPD insurances can be bought through a superannuation fund (even your own self-managed super fund) and are generally a tax deduction to the fund. Getting your life and TPD insurance here can make sense, as it will not affect your personal

(continued)

Structuring your life insurances—get proper advice *(cont'd)*

cashflow. If you are keen to make sure you don't eat up your super balance, you can usually contribute extra to super, possibly via salary sacrifice, to make sure their premiums are covered. There can be tax consequences of having your TPD insurance inside super—speak to a professional.

Trauma insurance cannot be purchased inside super and is not a tax deduction for you in your personal name. It needs to be purchased with after-tax money. But there is no tax to pay on a claim if you ever receive one.

Income protection can be purchased inside or outside of superannuation. However, the quality of cover offered inside super is inferior. It is never my preferred recommendation for clients. It is arguably the most important of all covers and the cover should be outside of super, where the quality of cover is better and the tax deductions are usually bigger.

Total and permanent disability insurance (TPD)

It's best to think of TPD insurance as major accident insurance. Essentially, you've had an accident and lost the use of your arms, legs or eyesight.

If that happens to you, how much money would you want to make the necessary changes to your life to cover the fact that you can't work anymore? Probably at least enough to cover all of your debts, *plus* a sum of money that will enable you to make some investments (including shares and/or property) that will replace the income that you won't be able to earn anymore.

For those with a home and even one investment property, a sum of more than $1 million might be required. For others with small children and significant property debt, it might be $2 million.

See the box entitled *Structuring your life insurances—get proper advice* for how TPD can be structured cash-flow effectively through super.

Trauma insurance

If TPD is major accident insurance, then trauma is major illness insurance. While the different policies can cover 30, 40 or 50 different conditions, the big ones are heart attack, cancer and stroke. Illnesses that in the 1970s might have killed you but, with modern medicine and technology, you now stand a better chance of 'stayin' alive'.

However, you might have massive medical bills (Medicare and the Pharmaceutical Benefits Scheme don't cover everything), or you might have to take six months or a year or two off work to recover. Trauma insurance is designed to give you money when you most need it. (I generally recommend about two years' worth of income or a minimum of $200 000 for clients, which would give them some financial security through most major illnesses.)

Income protection insurance

While life, TPD and trauma are lump sum payments—a defined event happens and agreed amount is paid out—income protection insurance is designed to provide you with an ongoing income stream if you are unable to work through injury or illness.

It is designed to cover up to 75 per cent of your main employment income, plus potentially further payments to your super fund to top up your super if you are unemployed for an extended period.

This is, arguably, the most important insurance, particularly for younger people buying property. If you are 35 and earning $100 000, you will earn around $3 million between now and age 65. That is what is going to pay for everything in your life, until your investment income from your property portfolio takes over, including your home, your holidays, cars, social life, the kids and their blasted school fees ...

So, if you could insure 75 per cent of your future income, wouldn't you? Your ability to earn an income is the biggest asset you own. And the premium is a tax deduction. It all adds up to a no-brainer—you need this and you need to speak to someone about taking it out.

Warning: The quality of cover offered inside superannuation is inferior. Take it outside of super if you can afford it, remembering it is a tax deduction.

How income protection can save your lifestyle

A client of mine had built up a portfolio of three properties, which necessarily included debt of more than $1 million. He was considerably negatively geared.

A distressing personal event led him into depression. He was struggling to work. Being self-employed, this meant he was only able to generate about half of the income that he previously had, for a period of about 18 months.

His income protection insurance, however, kicked in and saved him from losing everything. The insurance paid 75 per cent of the other half of the income that he wasn't able to earn, which gave him enough to hold on to the properties until he subsequently recovered.

Without the insurance, he would have, very quickly, lost all three properties.

This case was also an important reminder about why you take income protection insurance outside super, as income protection policies inside super are highly unlikely to cover you if you're able to work even part-time.

Getting ready for settlement

Depending on the settlement period you organised when you signed the contract, you will soon enter a countdown phase to ownership of your property.

For home buyers, you need to start to organise the packing of your current home, and getting the removalist ready (or hiring a truck). If you've been in your current home for a while, you might be surprised at how long it takes to pack up a house.

You will generally be permitted to do a final inspection of the property in the week before settlement occurs. Check things thoroughly. Disorganised vendors can leave a lot until the last minute, such as removing significant rubbish that they have collected over the years. If you are doing the inspection and you are concerned about the state of anything in the house, or you notice that details have changed from the time that you bought it, raise these concerns with the vendor's agent (who will usually accompany you on these inspections) and, if necessary, raise them with your solicitor to see if any action can be taken to ensure those items are dealt with before settlement.

For investors, as soon as you sign the contract, you should try to find yourself a real estate leasing agent to look after your property for you. Often, the vendor's agent will offer to do this for you, but you should meet with the agent and talk to other agents in the area, so that you make sure that the terms being offered by the agent — in terms of leasing and ongoing fees — are reasonable. In some cases, you might be able to have a tenant ready to move in the day after you take over the property.

Be aware that it's extremely rare for vacating vendors to leave the property in spic and span condition. In my experience, there's almost always a mess left behind that will need a few hours of cleaning up, either before you move in yourself or you show the house to potential tenants. Either leave yourself a few hours of scrubbing time, or organise a local contract cleaner to come in to give the house a once-over before you really start to make this place yours.

Last-minute finances

When settlement day is in sight, you will need to make sure the finances are in order.

About a week out from settlement, check with your bank or mortgage broker to make sure that there aren't going to be any last-minute hiccups. Most of the time there won't be, if you've got approval from your bank.

But strange things can happen … and those strange things have happened to me. When purchasing our second home, I checked with the bank every week from four weeks out that everything was in place. Three days before settlement, the bank claimed that there was a piece of paper that they now urgently needed signed by us. They said this could not be done and verified by the bank in time for settlement, which would have to be delayed. I was furious. I dealt firmly with the bank, letting them know that I had called every week and that this was now their problem, not mine. A manager made sure that this last-minute paperwork was received, dealt with, and that settlement occurred as planned.

Banks are big institutions and they're generally pretty efficient. But they do make mistakes, as do brokers and their clients (you). Work through the situation as calmly as you can, but understand that you need the right result and the best way of getting that is, generally, accepting that work needs to be done, someone needs to do it, and that helping rather than hindering the process is the most likely way that your outcome will be achieved.

Changing banking details

If you are getting your first loan, or moving to a new bank, you will need to change all of your banking details. Credit card payments and direct debits will need to be moved and this can be a painstaking process.

At some stage, go through your statements and write a list of the various institutions that you deal with. Then start making those changes, one by one, and crossing them off your list.

Change and check the addresses

There is a lot of paperwork involved in buying a property. Sometimes, it goes astray, or doesn't get done properly.

In the weeks and months after taking ownership of a property, you should check that you are receiving the right paperwork. Are you getting the rates for the new property? Is the bank sending details to the right address?

If you've moved house, have you told everyone that needs to know? With all of the paperwork that goes on, some things do get missed. It's happened to me twice and has cost me literally several thousands of dollars, due to errors that were clearly not mine. On both occasions, no matter that I could prove that the original error was made by someone else, it was deemed my responsibility to check these things to make sure that errors were corrected.

You're the customer and you deserve respect

The hassles involved means that nobody likes changing banks unless they have to. But when it comes to property ownership, keep in mind that banks are large institutions who will assume that you are happy unless you let them know otherwise.

If you've got a good relationship with your bank, then that's still no excuse not to make sure that they are treating you like a good customer.

Every few years, you should put your bank to the test. Check with your bank to see if you're on a good deal, particularly in regards to rates; check online or speak to a mortgage broker. If competitive forces have moved interest rates lower since you last looked at your loans, then you might be in a position to negotiate better rates.

Property purchasing principles

Buying a property comes with a big list of pre-purchase actions that need to be ticked off—it's unlike any other purchase you will ever make in your life. And given the money at stake—hundreds of thousands of dollars at a minimum—getting them wrong can dent or destroy your financial returns for a long time.

Don't skimp on these things. Get the lawyer to check over your contract. Get the building and pest inspections. Make sure you're aware of conditions on the sale or auction. Make sure you get sufficient insurances (both for the property itself and for you, personally).

If you are unsure of anything, hire some professional help, which can often include a lawyer, mortgage broker and real estate agent. Professionals do this work every day and they often only have to stop you making one mistake to have repaid whatever fee (or commission) that you have paid them. Though good professionals will often do far, far better than that with quality advice.

And once you've made your purchase, get ready for the enjoyment. Either enjoying the beautiful home you've just purchased, or the beautiful home you intend to turn it into. Or, if it's an investment, get ready for the money that a good purchase can, over time, make for you.

Best wishes for a profitable property future. If you'd like some help, I'm pretty easy to find!

And just to ram it home … here are the key points to take away from this chapter.

- Before signing the contract, you should conduct building and pest inspections, hire a conveyancer to help you with the paperwork, and look into any existing *subject to* clauses—or consider some of your own.

- Keep in mind that real estate agents' primary goal is to make the sale.

- Buyer's advocates can be extremely helpful in some cases.

- Auctions and private sales are the most common way property is sold in Australia; you can't put conditions of sale on a property bought at auction.

- Once your offer is accepted, you must organise insurance on your property.

- You should also consider insuring yourself in case anything unforeseen should happen that would affect the future of your family.

- When you're getting ready to settle on your purchase, confirm with the bank that everything is in order.

- If you are changing banks, ensure everything is in order with all associated paperwork and that your banking details are current for all your regular payments.

- Check your addresses on the paperwork and ensure they are up to date.

- If you have a good relationship with your bank, don't be afraid to ask for more competitive terms.

Bringing it all home

Move over dogs and diamonds, property is our real best friend.

It provides us with a roof over our heads. It's where we can watch our kids grow up. It's a place where you can relax and entertain and garden and barbecue.

But it's also a great investment asset class that is capable of helping you create enormous wealth over time, through a combination of rising income and capital growth.

I hope, dear reader, that you are now armed with what you need to know to get a great start on the 'Great Australian Dream' of property ownership, either as a home buyer or an investor. Or, if you've already bought some property, I hope I've helped you to fine-tune some skills that you've already had some practice with.

Property ownership is a source of pride, whether it's owning your own home (as most people want to do), or owning investment property (as almost as many people seem to want to do).

When you make the decision to buy property, it is usually one of the most exciting things to have happened in your life. It may well consume you for months leading up to the purchase and then for months or years after you finally succeed with a purchase and turn that piece of real estate into your *home*.

Wandering through open houses, imagining yourself in a place, where the furniture will be, how you'll improve the house, where the kids are going to sleep, the lifestyle that will come from living here (such as short walks to restaurants, parks, schools ...) is a thrill that can't be beaten.

And planning to strategically create for your future through property investment is, well...it's nearly as exciting. It can be every bit as consuming. Making sure that you get the first property purchase right can be crucial to whether you stop at one, or move on to build yourself a real property portfolio.

But don't get lost in the excitement or greed when it comes to the purchase, like the fat kid did when he fell into Willy Wonka's chocolate river. Too many people make too many mistakes when they buy property. And that can be financially devastating.

If you really want to make sure you give your property purchase the best chance of success, preparation is essential.

The really key messages that I want you to take away from this book are:

- Understand that a home and an investment property are very different purchases. Sure, they can both help you create substantial wealth, but that's not the primary aim of a home.

- A home should be an emotional purchase, where you buy a place that is going to make you happy and deliver a lifestyle that you desire.

- An investment property should be completely unemotional—it's about making money, pure and simple.

- Debt is simply a tool. It's not to be feared. It shouldn't keep you awake at night, like the head-spinning scene in *The Exorcist*. If you use it properly, it is a powerful ally in the game of wealth creation. And it comes part and parcel with property purchases. If you can learn to love debt—at least the okay and great kinds—you and debt can walk hand in hand as friends towards a more profitable future.

- Getting the debt right can add enormously (thousands of dollars a year) to the return the property will make you. Don't just go for the cheapest mortgage on the market. There are additional products, such as offsets and redraws, which can save, or make, you far more than a slightly lower interest rate with a lender that might not provide great support to your property ambitions.

- Before you buy, put thought into how you're going to own it (your holding structure) and how it's going to be funded (loan structure), as these are also significant factors that can enhance returns.

Last of all, I'd like to thank you for taking the time to read *Mortgages Made Easy*. As I said at the outset, good financial books have the potential to not only be good reads, but can literally make you thousands of dollars (or tens of thousands). If nothing else, I hope this book has given you ideas to help you do exactly that.

If you want further information, or believe that you could do with some help in implementing your property plans, then contact us at www.brucebrammallfinancial.com.au.

Or, if you'd like some ongoing free financial tidbits, or to read my monthly free newsletters, see the details in the following pages.

And, finally, I wish you the best with chasing your property dreams, whatever they may be. Whether it's finding and owning the perfect home sooner, or starting to build a portfolio, property is a wonderful, hands-on way to create wealth. I hope *Mortgages Made Easy* has made the lifelong task ahead a little easier for you.

Index

investment property *see also* debt;
loans; loan structure; mortgage;
property; property portfolios
—buying 99–129
—buying before a home
104–106
—buying first 17
—choice 13, 14–15, 93
—costs 14, 15
—loan structure 93, 100–101,
102–104, 105–109,
111–113
—maximising loans 109–111
—security 100–101, 102,
106–107, 152–154
—unemotional decision 13, 14,
25, 95, 99,165, 178
—value, increase in 16, 19–20
—wealth creation 16–23, 178

joint tenancy 132, 134, 139–140

lenders *see also* banks
—banks 50
—choice of 44–45, 50–52, 86
—multiple 152–153
—non-bank 50–51
—non-mainstream 30
lenders' mortgage insurance (LMI)
142, 29, 42, 75, 84–85, 100,
106, 157–159
leverage *see* debt; loans
lines of credit 66–67
loans, home *see also* debt;
finance structures; mortgage;
ownership structure
—aspects of 51–75
—construction 66

—first home 86–88
—interest only (I/O)
repayments 7, 35, 52, 55, 60,
76, 101, 102, 106, 110–111,
113, 128, 145, 147, 148,
149, 150
—multiple 112–113, 144–145
—principal and interest (P&I)
repayments 52–55, 76,
110–111, 119, 128, 146,
147, 148, 150
loan structure 93, 100–101,
102–104, 105–109, 111–113,
131–160, 178–179
—finance 7, 23–24, 132, 133,
142–159, 178
—importance of 131–132
—investment property
93, 100–101, 102–104,
105–109, 111–113
—ownership 7, 23–24, 132,
133–141, 179
—risks of poor 131–132,
134–135
loan-to-valuation ratio (LVR) 46,
75, 76, 85, 87, 107, 112, 113,
124, 155, 157–159

marshmallow experiment 9
mortgage (s) 49–76; *see also* debt;
loans; loan structure; loan to
valuation ratios; offset accounts;
interest rates; redraw accounts
—calculators 83
—choosing 7, 51–52
—credit cards 68–70
—exit fees 74
—fixed rates 7, 55, 56–57

**BRUCE
BRAMMALL
FINANCIAL**

Take *Mortgages Made Easy* one step further with Bruce Brammall Financial!

'If you think it's expensive to hire a professional, wait until you hire an amateur'.

The amateur most people hire is themselves.

Many people can D-I-Y their finances and do a very good job. You might be one of them, if you have the time, and the inclination, to learn to do things properly. There are many things I do myself because I can do a great job, *efficiently*. But boning up on some other topics to save a few bucks is something I choose not to do. Why? Because I'd rather kick a ball with my kids, or teach them a thing or two about life. I'd rather go on 'date night' with my wife. I'd rather read a book (or maybe even write another one), or catch up with a few mates to share a drink and watch the footy.

Your time is a limited commodity. It's your choice as to what you do and don't spend your precious time on. You can learn anything. But understand this: A professional will do in a few hours what it might take you dozens of hours to learn.

If you work too hard, if your time is too limited, if you'd simply rather not risk getting it horribly wrong by practicing on yourself... then contact Bruce Brammall Financial and get them to give you a hand. If you enjoyed this book, but not enough to go the extra yards to do the dozens of hours of research into your own position, then bring us in as part of your team of financial professionals.

I'd love to hear from you. And I'm sure the team at Bruce Brammall Financial could help.

We live and breathe finance. We've got decades of experience in the finance industry and can help you with everything from getting your first mortgage right and assisting you with general property advice, to helping protect your family and getting your superannuation and share portfolios running smoothly. (Sure, this is a book about property advice, but diversification is important and shares play an important role in that.)

What do we stand for? What do we pride ourselves on? The following are our values and they shine through in everything we do:

- Education

- Protection

- Simplicity

- Independence

- Fairness

- Leadership

- Wisdom

And what will you get when you attend your first meeting (in person, by Skype or by phone)? You'll get someone who will quickly be able to understand your unique situation and start to provide solutions to how your finances can be improved.

From that point, where the relationship goes is up to you.

If you're still unsure, dig around our website at www. brucebrammallfinancial.com.au. You can sign up for our free newsletters, register for our upcoming seminars and browse our extensive calculators to assist with some of your own research. And check the extensive library of my columns on almost every finance topic imaginable, for free.

I hope to meet you soon.

Bruce Brammall
www.brucebrammallfinancial.com.au
Email: bruce@brucebrammallfinancial.com.au
Phone: 03-9020-2905
Follow me: twitter@brucebrammall
google.com/+BruceBrammall

Connect *with* WILEY ▶▶▶

WILEY Browse and purchase the full range of Wiley publications on our official website.

www.wiley.com

 Check out the Wiley blog for news, articles and information from Wiley and our authors.

www.wileybizaus.com

 Join the conversation on Twitter and keep up to date on the latest news and events in business.

@WileyBizAus

 Sign up for Wiley newsletters to learn about our latest publications, upcoming events and conferences, and discounts available to our customers.

www.wiley.com/email

 Wiley titles are also produced in e-book formats. Available from all good retailers.

WILEY

Learn more with practical advice from our experts

Wrightbooks

Debt Man Walking
Bruce Brammall

**Australian Residential
Property Development
for Investors**
Ron Forlee

**Getting Started in Property
Investment For Dummies,
Australian Edition**
Bruce Brammall, Eric Tyson,
Robert S. Griswold

**Property Investing
For Dummies, 2nd
Australian Edition**
Bruce Brammall, Eric
Tyson, Robert S. Griswold

**Your Property Success
with Renovation**
Jane Slack-Smith

**Success as a Real Estate
Agent for Dummies,
Australian & New Zealand
Edition**
Terri M. Cooper, Dirk Zeller

**101 Ways to Save
Money on Your Tax —
Legally! 2014–2015**
Adrian Raftery

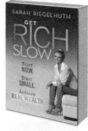

Get Rich Slow
Sarah Riegelhuth

Family Trusts 5E
N. E. Renton, Rod Caldwell

Available in print and e-book formats